To Anne,
Enjoy !

W9-CKE-578

Speeches
That Will
Leave Them
Speechless

& happy speaking
Kathryn McKenzie
Jan 2011

Speeches That Will Leave Them Speechless

An ABC Guide to Magnifying Your Speaking Success

KATHRYN MACKENZIE

FOREWORD BY CRAIG VALENTINE

Toronto and New York

Published in 2010 by
BPS Books
Toronto and New York
www.bpsbooks.com
A division of Bastian Publishing Services Ltd.

ISBN 978-1-926645-29-2

Cataloguing-in-Publication Data available from Library and Archives Canada.

Cover: Gnibel
Text design and typesetting: Casey Hooper Design

Printed by Lightning Source, Tennessee. Lightning Source paper, as used in this book, does not come from endangered old-growth forests or forests of exceptional conservation value. It is acid free, lignin free, and meets all ANSI standards for archival-quality paper. The print-on-demand process used to produce this book protects the environment by printing only the number of copies that are purchased.

TO MY DEAREST,
MOST LOVING MOTHER,

an unfailing source of inspiration and support
through my careers and life changes
and a superb role model of selfless giving from the heart
in order to be in service and better the lives of others.
Thank you for demonstrating firsthand that
the purpose of life is a life of purpose.

God bless you now and forever, Mom!

Contents

FOREWORD

by Craig Valentine

At the age of 10 I ran into my friend's father at the shopping mall and heard the words that changed the course of my life.

"You have a lisp," he said. "In fact, every time you open your mouth, you remind me of Daffy Duck."

This crushed me. Imagine if he could have fast-forwarded 18 years to see me standing on a stage in Chicago being crowned the 1999 World Champion of Public Speaking out of 175,000 Toastmasters in 68 countries and 25,000 contestants.

How did this happen? Well, you already know it couldn't have been my talent. So what was it? In a word: tools. I truly believe that successful speaking is 10% talent and 90% tools. But here's the tricky part: You have to have the *right* tools.

Some people think success in speaking is something you're born with or that you can master with practice. But let me ask you, "What if you're practicing the wrong things?"

I'm reminded of my daughter when she was eight months old. When she first learned to crawl, she crawled backwards. So guess what my wife and I did as parents? We put the TV remote control in front of her, because that was the one item she wanted most in life. And guess what she did? She crawled backwards faster! She had the ability but not the skill to grasp what was right in front of her.

This is exactly what happens to those who think they can practice blindly and become better speakers. If they use the wrong tools, they will only get better at getting worse. They'll go backwards faster. And even though the prizes of potential income, recognition, and rewards are directly in front of them, they won't be able to reach them. Plus, as they build these backward habits, it will become harder and harder for them to turn around and head in the right direction.

You must speak using the right tools if you want to make an impact. Again, it's not about talent, it's about tools.

"Where can I find these tools?" you may be wondering.

If you're looking for someone who has first-hand experience that will cut years off your learning curve and quickly turn you into the type of speaker who can keep your audiences on the edge of their seats, you've found her.

For years Kathryn MacKenzie has been putting together lessons to help people make rapid and tremendous growth in giving speeches, and now she has gathered all of these ideas into one place. *Speeches That Will Leave Them Speechless* is a one-stop shop for your speaking needs. If you master the concepts in this book, you will master the art of public speaking and you will be the kind of speaker others sign up and line up to see.

By the way, I can prove it. How? Well, the tools you will pick up in this book are the same tools I use every day of my speaking career. Without them, I'm lost. With them, I am found by others who want to hire me over and over again. Kathryn's tools will build your skills and magnify your magnificence as a speaker.

If I was able to go from Daffy Duck to World Champion to Professional Speaker using these tools, then what could you do with them? There's only one way to find out. Dive in and uncover this treasure-trove of invaluable concepts—concepts you won't find anywhere else. Then, when you come to the end of your speech, you'll look out at your audience and see their eyes filled with hope, feel the tremendous energy you just helped raise, and listen to their thunderous applause.

But when they approach you following your speech, don't be surprised that all the noise is gone. Chances are you've left them speechless.

Craig Valentine, MBA, is 1999 World Champion of Public Speaking, author of The Nuts and Bolts of Public Speaking, *co-author of* World Class Speaking, *founder of The Communication Factory, LLC, and co-founder of The World Class Speaking Coach Certification Program.*

ACKNOWLEDGMENTS

My heartfelt gratitude goes out to so many individuals and also to the organization of Toastmasters International for helping me develop as a speaker.

So very many wonderful people, in North America and around the world, too numerous for me to mention all of them individually, have helped me embark and forge ahead on this incredible seven-year journey to date. For the many speaking opportunities to grow as a keynote speaker and workshop facilitator, in both Canada and the United States, I thank you.

Most emphatically, I thank seven World Champions of Public Speaking, namely Ed Tate, Mark Brown, Randy Harvey,

David Brooks, Jim Key, and especially my constant mentors Darren LaCroix and Craig Valentine, for their outstanding instruction at Champ Camps and their invaluable educational resources.

Many, if not most, of the formulas that I teach in this book I picked up from Craig Valentine. I have found them to be very effective as I put them to the test in my instruction and coaching of others and in the creation and delivery of my keynote addresses.

Over the past five years, I have invested much of my time studying with Craig, most recently completing my certification in his online World Class Speaking course. My learning of the art of public speaking has increased tenfold through my attendance of many Champ Camps and my investment in Craig's many invaluable resources. Craig is truly a master teacher of public speaking. Not only does he have extensive knowledge of the subject, which he is continually upgrading, but he also has the superior skills to facilitate growth in others, regardless of the educational environment: virtually, in a physical class setting, or individually through his home-study resources. His vast knowledge has assisted me in writing this book, in writing on a multitude of topics for my monthly articles sent to my subscribers worldwide, and in developing content for my workshops on presentation skills. My confidence on the platform has been enhanced under

Craig's guidance. Consequently, I am repeatedly asked to be a keynote speaker at special events and conferences.

Thank you, Craig, for facilitating my growth as a speaker. Because of what I have learned from you about the art of public speaking, I have received recognition and respect in the speaking world. Most importantly, Craig, thank you for being my role model as a person whose mission is to touch lives ... May I always keep this goal in my mind and heart as I attempt to do the same in my own unique way.

FOUR A'S TO
ANCHOR YOUR POINTS

> **"What's loose is lost
> and what's tight
> stays in sight."**

—Craig Valentine,
1999 World Champion of Public Speaking

When was the last time you heard a speech that needed to be tighter? As a result, the message was quickly lost and forgotten. Was it your speech? It's likely that we've all been there and done that, right?

> **PROMISE:** By tying your point(s) to one or more anchors, depending on the time allotted for your talk, your speech will be tighter, your message will be more memorable, and you will be in greater demand as a speaker.

> **ROADMAP:** According to master teacher, coach, and mentor Craig Valentine, there are four ways to anchor a point. We'll look at all four.

The key to a memorable takeaway message is to anchor it to one of the Four A's and to follow that with a solid foundational phrase (message) that people can clearly remember and repeat. (See pages 43–48 for an in-depth look at foundational phrases.) Examples of these phrases are:

- Walk Your Talk

- How to Affect Not Infect Others

- To Gain You Need to Feel the Pain

Four A's to Anchor Your Points

1. **Anecdote:** a story. A personal story that taught you a life lesson is the most important anchor. Stories make points stick. When your listeners remember your story, they remember your point.

2. **Analogy:** the use of comparison. Compare something with which a general audience is familiar to something they may not know. This clarifies the point succinctly and precisely. If a picture says a thousand words, then an analogy shows a thousand pictures. For example:

- A speaker compares the experience of immediate, unexpected change in our lives to what householders go through after a hurricane

- Speaker Peter Legge compares our life journey to a runway at an airport. The tarmac *will* run out, he says, so we need to value and make the best of our time while we're on it

3. **Acronym:** a new word created by using the first letter of each word in a phrase. Acronyms help people remember a formula and/or a process. Some speakers use acronyms in their roadmap at the start of their speech.

Do you remember a teacher using the acronym HOMES to help you remember the names of the five Great Lakes?

Are you familiar with the acronym LOL, used online to represent Laugh Out Loud?

A speaker helping people aspire to greater heights might suggest that they invest in TEA—the qualities necessary to reach their potential: Tenacity, Enthusiasm, and Attitude. Isn't it easier for people to remember steps or points when they can call an acronym back to memory?

4. **Activity:** There's time in a 45- to 60-minute keynote to involve the audience in an activity or two. Activities give an audience a kinesthetic experience, helping them learn by doing. Activities are appropriate ways to drive home a point, as long as they are brief and relevant, and add value. Don't forget to follow an activity with a debriefing time so your audience grasps the full value of the activity.

Mixing anchors in your content provides variety, holds your audience's interest, and helps them remember your point or message.

Before and after anchors, use reflective, open-ended questions (who, what, when, where, why questions). Give the audience quiet times to ponder and be introspective. Remember: "Wisdom comes from reflection" (Patricia Fripp).

Next time you speak, tighten your speech by anchoring your points so they will be remembered and repeated.

From Boring
to Brilliant

"IT IS CRIMINAL TO BE BORING!"

–ED TATE, CSP
2000 WORLD CHAMPION OF PUBLIC SPEAKING

"NEVER BE BORING AGAIN!"

–DOUG STEVENSON,
SPEAKER AND AUTHOR

It's safe to assume that we've all glazed over during certain speeches. Worse still, most of us, on occasion, have looked out and seen a glazed-over look in our audience's eyes.

PROMISE: Commit yourself to going from boring to brilliant and you will look out on interested, enthused, engaged faces, instead of a room full of screensaver eyes.

ROADMAP: To commit to being brilliant as a speaker, examine both the *ways to be boring* and the *ways to be brilliant* sections that follow and determine which speaking techniques you need to change in order to enhance your speaking level—techniques related to your:

- Structure

- Content

- Delivery

Ways to Be Boring

Your Structure

- Open with unpleasant pleasantries, e.g., nice to be here, lovely weather, etc.

- Squeeze in too much information; this creates rambling on your part and confusion in your audience's minds

Your Content

- Present a loosely organized message that leaves the audience lost, confused, bored, zoned out

- Never use humor

- Tell all your stories as narratives, using the third person

- Tell stories that make you appear superior, special, one of a kind. If your audience cannot relate to you and your stories, they will lose hope that they can better themselves and their lives

- Give a data dump or a PowerPoint parade. Left-brain, linear, logical points may be filled with interesting facts, but they are usually boring and leave audiences thinking: So what! Who cares? What's in it for me?

Your Delivery

- Speak in the same tone, pace, volume—show no emotions. "Sameness is the enemy of the speaker," Patricia Fripp says

- Lip-synch with slides

- Never smile

- Move around without purpose

WAYS TO BE BRILLIANT

Your Structure

- Open with a bang. Remove all distractions with a strong opening; frame your message clearly by getting right into the content with your promise of how your audience will benefit from what they will hear; provide a roadmap of where you'll be taking them

- Structure your content so your points are both clear and palatable and your takeaway message is doable

Your Content

- Know your message and be able to say it in fewer than 10 words. Be concise and precise in describing your message

- Let them laugh at you, with you. People love to hear and laugh at others' Five F's: their Firsts, Flaws, Fears, Failures, and Frustrations. Remember: When people laugh, they relax; when they relax, they learn; when they learn, they remember

- Tell simple, everyday stories that have taught you life lessons/processes from which they too can learn. By making yourself similar to them, you will connect and make yourself endearing to them

- Use characters and dialogue. Make your characters the heroes; give them the best lines about the lessons you have learned

- Learning requires the whole-brain approach—using both left and right lobes. Allow for humor, spontaneity, emotion, and creativity along with your use of facts, quotations, and statistics. As speaker Doug Stevenson says: "Emotion is the fast lane to the brain. Speak from your head with your heart wide open." People are moved to action emotionally, not intellectually

Your Delivery

- By using characters and dialogue, you will naturally and automatically have vocal variety. L. Heckler says that speakers should relive their stories rather than just retell them

- Never read slides. Use less text and more graphics. A picture is worth a thousand words

- Smile and your audience will smile back

- Move with purpose on the platform (see pages 193–200 for details)

Yes, indeed, it is criminal to be Boring, so commit to being Brilliant.

CREATE COMPELLING CONTENT THAT CONNECTS

"AUDIENCES DON'T CARE
HOW MUCH YOU KNOW;
THEY WANT TO KNOW
HOW MUCH YOU CARE."

–ZIG ZIGLAR,
SPEAKER AND AUTHOR

"THE WORDS 'INFORMATION'
AND 'COMMUNICATION'
ARE OFTEN USED
INTERCHANGEABLY.
INFORMATION IS GIVING OUT,
WHILE COMMUNICATION
IS GETTING THROUGH."

–SYDNEY J. HARRIS,
JOURNALIST AND AUTHOR

A speech should feel like a conversation between two friends, the audience and the speaker. For a congenial conversation to occur, the speaker must create a connection. A connection is established on two levels: the emotional and the intellectual. Great speeches use feelings and logic, heart and head. Lead with the right side of the brain (the emotional) and follow with the left (the intellectual).

PROMISE: For change to occur in the listeners' thoughts, feelings, words, or actions, a speaker has to tap not only into their intellect but more importantly into their emotions. A human connection requires a degree of caring, sincerity, and empathy, demonstrating attitudes such as: "I've been there, too"; "I understand how you felt"; "I can relate to that experience, too."

ROADMAP: I will use the PARTS Formula to demonstrate how you can create compelling content that connects with your audiences. This formula can serve as a checklist for you when you're creating content. Content is *what* you say.

Here's the most important question you need to ask yourself before you start writing your speech: What would I like my audience to think, feel, say, or do *differently* after I speak?

The PARTS Formula: How to Connect Using Compelling Content

When it comes to content, work on going narrow and deep into a topic.

Most presenters use only one or two elements of the PARTS Formula. World class speakers use at least four and sometimes even all five for each point they make.

P = Phrase

I'm talking here about your foundational phrase—your audience's takeaway message.

The foundational phrase is the most important part of your speech. (Please see pages 43–48 for more details on foundational phrases.)

Your phrase must be brief—*fewer* than 10 words. It must be you-focused, because it's all about them, the audience, not you, the speaker. It should be a simple, catchy, repeatable phrase or sentence, as in, "A Phrase That Pays" (Doug Stevenson). Here are some other examples:

- Be driven by your vision

- Your attitude toward anything is everything

- If you can see it, you can be it

- Lasting change is gradual change

- View obstacles as stepping stones, not stumbling blocks

Reflect with your audience on why your phrase is important to you personally.

A = Anchor

There are four main kinds of anchors that will help your points stick in your audience's minds: anecdote (story), analogy, acronym, and activity. An anchor is whatever you tie your point to so it can be remembered. (See pages 1–6 above for more details about Anchors.)

R = Reflection

What question can you ask to get your audience thinking about their own situation as it relates to your point? Come up with a bold statement you can make about this point and then embed it into a scenario, real or hypothetical, in which the audience can actually see themselves.

The best reflection questions are open-ended—Who, What, When, Where, Why questions. For example:

"Who was the person who influenced you to ...?"

"What was it that ...?"

"When was the last time you ...?"

"Where were you when ...?"

People need to hear not only your voice but also their inner voice, since, as Patricia Fripp says, "Wisdom comes from reflection."

T = Technique

Give your audience a tangible technique to do, rather than just asking them to think or feel. Provide them with a doable technique that will take them on a better life path. For example, you could say:

- Write down your perfect day

- Change your language

- Stay away from the crabs in a barrel

- Hang around with positive people

- Follow your kids around with a notebook; they are great sources of humor

- Share your Five F's—your Firsts, Flaws, Fears, Failures, and Frustrations—because empathetic humor is the cheapest and most abundant gift you can give to others

S = Sale

Why should your audience members take your advice on this point? What's in it for them? What are the consequences if they don't take heed and the rewards if they do? You can use the Sale to agitate your audience members to want to alter their current situation and better their lives. This is an art form in itself, one that must be mastered if you're going to create world class speeches.

Using the EDGE Sales Formula will help you motivate everyone in your audience. EDGE stands for the benefits they will receive by taking your advice:

E ... Higher Esteem

D ... Doing More

G ... Gaining More

E ... Enjoying More

As you promote the EDGE benefits, you need to state not only what your audience wants to attain, but also what they want to avoid. "Push them into the pull. Make them sick to make them better" (Craig Valentine).

Use If ... then ... statements.

*If you don't ... then ... (loss or consequence). State what they want to **avoid**.*

*But if you do ... then ... (gain or benefit). State what they want to **attain**.*

For example:

> *If you choose to adopt a negative attitude, you'll infect people and as a result repel them. That means you'll be isolated from others and lonely; you likely will never reach your professional goals, either.*

> *On the other hand, if you choose to adopt a positive attitude, you will affect people with joy. They will be drawn to you like a magnet. You'll revel in the happiness of personal and professional successes.*

A word of warning: When you use the PARTS Formula, remember not to put yourself on a pedestal. Make yourself similar to your audience by sharing your Five F's (your Firsts, Flaws, Fears, Failures, Frustrations). This will endear you to your audience. They will readily relate to you as a human being with frailties similar to their own.

DELIVER THREE KINDS
OF DIALOGUE

"THE HEART OF A SPEECH
IS A STORY; THE HEART OF A
STORY IS DIALOGUE."

–CRAIG VALENTINE,
1999 WORLD CHAMPION OF PUBLIC SPEAKING

"DON'T *RETELL* THE STORY,
RELIVE IT!"

–MARK BROWN,
1995 WORLD CHAMPION OF PUBLIC SPEAKING

Speaker Patricia Fripp says when you fail to use dialogue, "you're really not telling a story, you're simply giving a report." If you use the third-person narrative format, your speeches will become lengthy, impersonal, and lifeless. The result will be a bored, disengaged audience.

PROMISE: Balance narrative with dialogue in your stories and you will draw your audience into your scenes—they will actually *relive* them with you in the present. You are much more likely to create an interested, connected, engaged audience.

ROADMAP: There are three different types of dialogue:

- Character-to-Character Dialogue

- Inner Dialogue

- Audience Dialogue

CHARACTER-TO-CHARACTER DIALOGUE

If any form of dialogue is used, this is the most common one. It involves hypothetically bringing another character into your stories and giving them a voice by stating their exact spoken words.

Tips for Using Character-to-Character Dialogue:

1. Be believable by having characters act and react with emotion and body language to specific situations in your stories. Demonstrate a rollercoaster series of emotions.

2. Have the dialoguing characters use each other's names in their conversation so it's clear to the audience who is speaking.

3. Use vocabulary normally used by the characters you have chosen—for example, appropriate to age. Modulate your voice to differentiate between yourself and your character.

4. To uncover humor, instead of adding it, let it evolve

from the dialogue. Add facial expressions as reactions to spoken lines or events in your story.

5. Be careful to balance dialogue and narrative; too much dialogue creates a play.

6. Step out of the scene and talk to your audience to draw the point out of your story.

7. Use dialogue to have a character pass on a process, lesson, or wisdom to be learned by the audience. Never make yourself the guru if you want to endear yourself to your audience. Give another character the best lines and ensure that it is he or she who imparts the wisdom, not you.

A word of warning: If you're taking on the role and dialogue of a different gender in your speech, do not try to achieve female and male vocal pitches; this may end up being comedic and obscure your message. Simply alter your voice slightly so your audience gets the difference.

INNER DIALOGUE

This type of dialogue allows the audience to actually *hear* your thoughts.

Your audience will connect with you when they hear your innermost feelings before, during, and after the process/lesson you experienced in resolving a problem, overcoming an obstacle, or arriving at a solution. For example:

"I thought: Isn't that amazing? After so long, I ..."

"My mind kept churning all the information over and over. Oh, what shall I do? Then suddenly, the decision came to me ..."

Speak from your heart, not your head. You may need to go to the edge with your emotions, but make sure you come back to centre yourself again. Your words, tone, and body language must be congruent with one another.

AUDIENCE DIALOGUE

This type of dialogue gives the audience a voice and helps them to be heard. "People buy into what they help create," as Craig Valentine says.

Create opportunities for your audience to say/repeat/re-cap your main points. That way they'll be more likely to buy into and remember your message. Greater interaction also results in a deeper connection between you and them.

If you want them to take part orally, you must train them to do so early in the speech; otherwise they will not feel at ease participating later.

For example, get your audience to:

- Complete a sentence or phrase

- Repeat something after you

- Summarize your speech's takeaway message

Have them pair off to discuss a question. You could make one person a star or make the audience a character so you can give them dialogue

Want to make them laugh? Read their minds.

- Anticipate what they may be thinking

- Tell them you know what they're thinking

- Then tell them exactly what they're thinking

Which of the three types of dialogue have you avoided? Which will you try to use in your next speech or presentation?

ENGAGE YOUR AUDIENCE
AS AN EDUTAINER

"Make sure you have finished speaking before your audience has finished listening."

–Dorothy Sarnoff,
singer, actress, and speaker

"When you speak, take them on a rollercoaster ride of emotions."

–Doug Stevenson,
speaker and author

Do effective speakers engage audiences intellectually with statistics, facts, and figures? I'm hoping you responded: "No, they don't, because effective speakers are aware that people are never moved to action intellectually. People are moved to action emotionally."

A speech is composed of three elements—structure, content, and delivery.

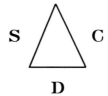

In planning and presenting the triangle, effective speakers make sure the audience is emotionally engaged throughout.

PROMISE: If you work hard on only one or two parts of the triangle, your presentation will fall below average and you may even lose your audience. But if you work hard on all three parts, you'll be strides ahead of other speakers. You and your message will be memorable. As a result, you'll move audiences to action so they can better their lives.

ROADMAP: Let's look at six do's and don'ts (grouped under the topics of Structure, Content, and Delivery) so you can see how to engage your audiences emotionally.

DON'T

Structure

1. Don't miss the opportunity to grab their attention at the start.

   • Don't state unpleasant pleasantries. e.g., "Great to be here." "Wonderful weather we're having," etc.

2. Don't write a nine-minute speech and try to squeeze it into seven. If you squeeze too much information into your speech, you'll squeeze your audience out.

Content

3. Don't be unclear regarding your message.

- Don't make the audience figure it out on their own; you'll risk losing them on the way

- Don't confuse your audience when you're trying to have them buy into your point; a confused mind always says no

4. Don't make it all about you, the speaker, or use third-party stories exclusively rather than some of your own. They will think: "So what? Who cares? What's in it for me? There's nothing here for me." Result? They will zone out.

Delivery

5. Don't talk *at* the audience.

- Don't pontificate

- Don't be superior or special, or come across as a know-it-all

- Don't make yourself the hero or guru with all the answers

6. Don't remain at the same energy level. "Sameness is the enemy of the speaker," as Patricia Fripp says. The audience will become bored and zone out whether the problem is sameness in your voice (volume, rate, pitch), sameness in body language, or sameness in stage movement/non-movement. Be careful, though, and avoid being constantly dynamic, because that would be sameness, too. "Those who sleep in noise, awake in silence," Craig Valentine says.

DO

Structure

1. Do have them at "hello."

  • Smile and make eye contact

  • Open with a bang: a question, story, statistic, or quotation

2. Do write a five-minute speech and say it in seven.

  • This gives you time to connect with your audience through questions and pauses so they can be silent, reflect, and hear their own inner voice

Content

3. Do be very clear about your message.

    - Be able to say it in fewer than 10 words ("walk your talk"; "success is not a given")

    - Know exactly what you want the audience to think, feel, or do differently after you finish speaking

4. Do make it all about them, the audience.

    - Use I-focused stories and you-focused messages. At the start, frame your message and its benefits; connect with the audience throughout by using rhetorical questions, eye contact, and the most important connective word, *you*

Delivery

5. Do talk *with* the audience.

    - Be conversational

    - Make someone else or the process you learned the hero

- Draw on your similarities with your audience by being humble/human, discussing one or a few of your Five F's: your Firsts, Flaws, Fears, Failures, Frustrations

6. Do alter your energy levels throughout.

- Exercise your Four P's: alter your Pace, Pitch, and Projection and introduce Pauses to fit the moments you have reached in a speech:

  - The seriousness or levity of a story

  - The mood of the characters within the story

  - An event you are describing

Make sure your voice and body language are congruent with the words you're speaking and appropriate to the content of what you're saying or describing. Use a different tone when stepping out of your story and making a point to the audience.

Be an Edutainer

Your main purpose in speaking is to change the audience's thinking and feeling about a topic you believe is important. The reason you need to appeal to both their intellect and their emotions is that you want them to think, feel, speak, and act differently after you finish speaking.

Just because you say something doesn't mean the audience will remember it. As a speaker, don't you want your message to be remembered and repeated?

In their role as educators, speakers teach lessons and raise their audience's level of consciousness to positively affect their lives. Educators take life lessons they have learned from others, personal stories, and events and share them with others for their own growth.

In their role as entertainers, speakers connect with the audience, bringing levity, amusement, and laughter to the proceedings; otherwise the audience ends up with "screen-saver eyes."

The most effective speakers, therefore, are "edutainers."

To edutain doesn't mean you have to have the audience rolling in the aisles with laughter; your goal is to amuse with some occasional levity in stories and examples, producing laughter or simply smiles. Amusement lightens up serious speeches, breaks monotony, and energizes both you and your audience.

Darren LaCroix sums it all up this way: "Do you want your audience to remember your important message? Do you want to maintain their interest throughout your speech? Do you want to make a difference in their lives? Remember: 'When people laugh or are being amused, they relax; when they relax, they learn; when they learn, they remember.' "

Most of all, share a lesson, have fun, go on a journey, and take the audience with you by giving your speech a solid structure, compelling content, and a dynamic delivery.

Your Speech's
Foundational Phrase

"YOUR VERY CLEAR MESSAGE IS THE FOUNDATION UPON WHICH EVERYTHING ELSE IS BUILT ... WITHOUT THE FOUNDATIONAL MESSAGE —YOU ARE BUILDING A CASTLE ON QUICKSAND. IT WILL NOT SURVIVE AND YOUR MESSAGE WILL SINK INTO OBSCURITY. YOU WILL PROBABLY SINK WITH IT."

—CRAIG VALENTINE,
1999 WORLD CHAMPION OF PUBLIC SPEAKING

Have you ever considered why many speakers confuse and lose their audiences? You may say it's because they don't speak with conviction, or have poor body language, or don't connect by involving the audience.

Although these points are valid, they are definitely *not* the main reason. The main reason these speakers lose their audiences is that they themselves are lost; they have not done the necessary preliminary mental work to formulate a solid, foundational phrase or crystal-clear takeaway message as the basis of their speech.

> **PROMISE:** You will be considered a high-caliber speaker when you formulate a very clear, concise message for each speech, one that serves as the foundation of all the points in your speech. Your audiences will be inspired to follow you because your message will be memorable.

> **ROADMAP:** We will examine a speech's Foundational Phrase by looking at the important questions you need to ask yourself when you're beginning to create your speech. Then we'll look at an analogy for further clarification.

Important Questions to Ask Yourself

So you have a speech or presentation to prepare!

- You've already determined the makeup and needs of your target audience

- You know it's important for you to create compelling, relevant content for this audience

- You don't know exactly where to start

Start by creating a crystal-clear *Foundational Phrase*, which is, in fact, the takeaway message you wish to give your audience.

Ask yourself the following questions to ensure that your foundational phrase is crystal clear and concise for both you and your audience:

1. What do I want my audience to think, feel, say, or do differently after I finish speaking?

2. What is the takeaway message—the foundational phrase—for my audience?

3. Is it clear, feasible, palatable, and doable for my audience?

4. Can I say it in fewer than 10 words?

5. Is it you-focused?

6. Have I found a way to state it in a creative, possibly rhythmic way—as a "phrase that pays" (Doug Stevenson)? For example:

   The Thrill of Soaring Starts with the Fear of Falling

   Attitude Determines Altitude

   Dream, Decide, and Do

   Nothing Changes Unless Someone Changes

7. Once I've decided on a clear message, which stories (humorous or otherwise) or other anchors and other supporting points can I use to get my message across and make it easy to remember?

A Clarifying Analogy

Here's an analogy that may clarify this extremely important point of creating a foundational phrase and its supporting points.

Imagine the foundational phrase of your speech as a coat rack. It stands solid and grounded.

The supporting points to get your message across are the coats you hang on the hooks of the coat rack. Make sure all of your supporting points—benefits, stories, activities, acronyms, analogies, humor, techniques you give an audience, questions you ask the audience—are clearly related to the foundational phrase. "The phrase determines what stays."
(Craig Valentine)

Drop off the hooks and onto the floor whatever doesn't support your main message. "When in doubt, leave it out!"
(Craig Valentine)

Next time you have a speech or presentation to prepare, make sure you have a crystal-clear foundational phrase, one that is fewer than 10 words. Focus on it. When you do, your mind will attract points to support it. Compile all ideas by recording them; discard the ones that are not needed.

Don't worry that this process will inundate you with a multitude of thoughts, ideas, and stories. Before you create a message, you first need to create a mess. If you have a huge mess, you're on the right track to formulating a great message.

GENERATE GENUINE GESTURES

"WHEN DELIVERING A
SPEECH, BE NATURAL
BUT ENLARGED."

–DALE CARNEGIE,
MOTIVATIONAL AUTHOR AND SPEAKER

"THE BELIEVABILITY OF
WHAT WE COMMUNICATE IS
INFLUENCED 7% BY WORDS,
38% BY TONE OF VOICE AND
55% BY BODY LANGUAGE.
IN OTHER WORDS, 93% OF
THE MESSAGE IS CONVEYED
USING 'PARALANGUAGE.'"

–DR. ALBERT MEHRABIAN,
SILENT PASSAGES

Have you ever heard speakers utter words that are out of synch with their facial expression? They may say how thrilled they are to be there but forget to inform their own face of that fact. As a result, you don't believe what they say. Nonverbal communication has a greater impact than we may like to imagine. Most communication comes not from what we say, but from how we say it.

PROMISE: When you place as much effort on mastering the art of delivery as on setting up a solid structure and creating compelling content, you will communicate effectively, connect deeply, and hold your audience's attention. The secret to mastering your delivery is to master the *nonverbal* aspects of speaking through genuine gestures.

ROADMAP: Because our bodies speak volumes, we will examine how *body is language*, by looking at the *what*, the *why*, and the *how* of using gestures.

Great speakers "handshake" with their audience. They use embracing gestures that say, "I like you."

Do you like them? Do your gestures say so?

What Is a Gesture?

A gesture is a movement of the body or part of the body (hand gestures and facial expressions) to express or emphasize ideas, emotions, and intentions. You want your audience to receive your intended message; no gestures, or the wrong gestures, however, will confuse their minds. The most effective use of gestures is based on congruency between the words you utter and the movement and/or emotion demonstrated by your body.

As much as you work hard to have control over your verbal messages, doesn't it make sense to have equal control over your nonverbal messages—your gestures?

Use gestures sincerely, naturally, and smoothly, just as you do when you are in a conversation with someone. The larger the audience, the more enlarged you become. Be careful not to lose your naturalness, sounding like speaker man or speaker woman and appearing fake, contrived, and insincere. Also be careful not to point at the audience, getting into a preaching mode; they will feel you are talking down to them.

WHY AND HOW TO USE GESTURES

Why Use Gestures?

Gestures appeal to the three styles by which people learn:

- Visual: learning best through images

- Auditory: learning best through listening

- Kinesthetic: learning best through experiencing

Gestures give your point a stronger impact, especially when you're doing a good job of connecting and bonding with members of your audience.

Gestures strengthen the audience's understanding of your point.

Gestures add to your message.

Gestures add concreteness—for example by indicating size, height, or distance.

Gestures, along with the accompanying characters' dialogue, help you relive your stories rather than just retelling them in narrative form.

How to Use Gestures

- Use gestures to paint pictures for visual learners so they can visualize the scene

- Use gestures to stress the spoken words for auditory learners

- Use gestures to add to the emotion and feelings in your speech for kinesthetic learners

When emphasizing or stating an important point, pause and speak more slowly and in a lower voice, making sure your facial expression is sincere; let your eyes linger on an individual for a few seconds while delivering your entire phrase or sentence, then move on.

Use your arms, hands, fingers.

Include characters, dialogue, and use of natural, though enlarged, conversational gestures.

When it comes to gestures, the key to success is to let yourself relax and respond naturally to what you're thinking, feeling, and saying. And remember, even when you're not saying anything, you're still communicating a message. *Body is language.*

I challenge you to become more aware of what your body language is expressing. Videotape yourself speaking in front of an audience so you can observe how others see you. The camera doesn't lie. You'll be able to see both your good habits and your bad ones. Turn off the sound and watch yourself in action.

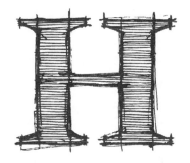

HOOK ONTO HUMOR

"Don't add humor,
uncover it."

–Craig Valentine,
1999 World Champion of Public Speaking

"Use the 4 H's in your
speeches: Head, Heart,
Humor, and ...
a Heavy-duty message."

–Ed Tate, CSP,
2000 World Champion of Public Speaking

"When you humorize,
you humanize."

–Darren LaCroix,
2001 World Champion of Public Speaking

Humor is the cheapest, most abundant gift you can give to others. Hook onto it by recalling your own funny or even embarrassing stories, and then share them with your audience.

An interesting exchange took place at one of Patricia Fripp's weekend seminars in Las Vegas on presentation skills.

"Do I really have to be funny or entertaining?" a new speaker asked.

"Only if you want to get paid!" Patricia responded.

PROMISE: Highly esteemed speakers don't need to be standup comics to hold an audience's attention, but they do need to be entertaining. Using humor, just like giving a speech itself, is a process that can be learned. It takes new tools, practice (in front of real audiences), and time. How can you be funnier if you aren't yet comfortable in front of an audience? The more you practice with the right tools, the more comfortable you will become, and the more comfortable you become, the more effective you will be.

ROADMAP: This chapter delves into:

- Secrets of the trade that require practice

- A few *don'ts* when you're trying to be humorous

"But I'm not a comedian. Can I still be funny and make people laugh?" you may ask. Even if you don't have your audience rolling in the aisles with laughter, you can definitely learn to be entertaining, and, with extra effort, even funny. Remember, however, that forced, contrived humor is usually worse than no humor at all.

As Craig Valentine reminds us, do not add humor to your speeches, but uncover it from within. Draw it out of your stories, characters, and their dialogue.

A FEW SECRETS OF THE TRADE

COMEDY IS A PROCESS

As stated above, comedy is a process that can readily be learned by anyone.

It takes knowing and using comedic tools and techniques, practicing in front of audiences, and time.

BODY IS LANGUAGE

Act and react, using your emotions. Don't talk and tell but share and show, using gestures, facial expressions, vocal variety (via the Four P's—Projection, Pace, Pitch, Pauses), and the voice of your characters.

FACTS TELL, STORIES SELL

Tell personal stories (though they don't have to be Hollywood blockbusters). Make fun of yourself, not others (use your own embarrassing stories).

COMEDY STEMS FROM TRAGEDY

Share your Five F's:
Firsts, Flaws, Fears, Failures, Frustrations.

UNEXPECTED TWISTS

People laugh when their minds are tricked. "I was so nervous about the trip, I took a blanket, a flashlight and … PAUSE … my mother!" (Darren LaCroix). The punch word comes last.

REACTIONS CREATE HUMOR

React with facial expressions that fit what you're saying. Use appropriate timing by pausing, delivering the punch-line, giving the look . . . then shutting up to let the audience laugh.

POWER OF THREE'S

Derail your audience's thoughts. For example, Darren La-Croix sometimes tells a Toastmasters audience that he prefers them over audiences in comedy clubs because "you're so attentive, so supportive, and so .... sober." Setup, setup . . . punch word.

READ YOUR AUDIENCE'S MIND

Read the minds of your audience. Tell them what they're actually thinking after you set up information that causes them to figure out something. For example, you state something you experienced as a 20-year-old. You also state the year of the experience. This limited information will naturally get them trying to figure out your current age. You then can interrupt their thoughts by saying: "Okay, okay, I know you're doing the math ... carry 1 ... take away 3 ... She must be ..."

CHARACTERS

Let your characters be:

- Seen (give physical descriptors)

- Known (relate a brief back story)

- Heard (put it into dialogue)

AND, IN ADDITION . . .

- Odd not even numbers are funnier

- Specific not generic brands are funnier

- Expressing inner dialogue (your own thoughts) can be extremely funny

- Exaggeration is not only accepted in comedy, it is expected

DON'TS WHEN USING HUMOR

- Don't recycle jokes and stories

- Don't laugh throughout your story, especially before delivering the punch-line

- Don't deliver a story too quickly or not loudly enough

- Don't slip out of character when telling a story

- Don't step on your laughs—allow them the time to laugh

- Don't give yourself as a character in your story the best laughter lines

- Don't add humor; *uncover* it in your stories, characters, and dialogue

- Don't be politically incorrect

If you take one major lesson or point from this chapter, let it be this one:

Don't *add* humor; *uncover* it in your own stories, characters, and their dialogue, giving characters other than yourself the best lines.

I leave you with a statement from Darren LaCroix: "When people laugh, they relax, when they relax, they learn, when they learn, they remember."

Do *you* want people to remember what you said?

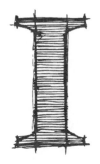

IGNITE YOUR AUDIENCE WITH A GREAT INTRODUCTION

"Here's one thing I know for sure: once I changed my introduction from 'me' focused to 'you' focused, I gave myself an extreme advantage before I ever said one word. The same thing can happen to you too."

–Craig Valentine,
1999 World Champion of Public Speaking

Have you ever heard a speaker being introduced by another and thought:

- All these accomplishments are great but they sound so boastful

- What's the relevance of these credentials to the topic of the speech?

- There's no mention of any benefit(s) for us, the audience

- So what? Who cares? What's in it for me?

Effective speakers always write their own inroductions and give them, ahead of time, to the organizers where they're going to be speaking. The introduction you give them "flavors your entire speech ... and gets the audience fired up and excited," as Craig Valentine says.

When an intro to a speaker is self-focused, the audience is justified in assuming that the entire speech is going to be about the speaker with little or nothing for them. This kind of introduction turns an audience off before the speaker even says a word. A great introduction is worth its weight in gold when it comes to creating a connection with audiences.

PROMISE: By creating introductions that focus on *them*, the audience, rather than on *you*, the speaker, you will help your organizers establish a positive tone and put the audience in a receptive mood. Most importantly, such an introduction will ignite the audience, energizing them and making them eager to hear you speak.

ROADMAP: Craig Valentine has taught "How to Ignite Your Audience" by using skillfully prepared and delivered introductions. Below is a summary of Craig' five steps; the examples are from the introductions I have given to those who introduce me.

FIVE STEPS FOR CREATING IMPACTFUL INTRODUCTIONS FOR YOUR ORGANIZERS

1. **Start off making it about them by using a question(s) or a statement(s) with as many "you" words as you can.**

For example, "Have you ever gone into screensaver mode when listening to a speech? Have you ever given one of those speeches? On the other hand, have you ever been captivated by a speaker from the start to the finish of the speech? What is the difference that makes the difference?"

2. **Make a promise, indicating the benefits they will receive.**

"Today you will discover three essential speaking keys that not only will remove you from where most speakers are—in the wannabe speaker group—but also will provide you with the tools and techniques needed for you to be held in high esteem and be in demand as a world-class speaker."

3. **Include only the credentials that are relevant to your topic.**

If I am talking to a group of teachers, whether retired or still teaching, I mention my many years as an educator because my time in that profession aligns me to them by making me similar, not special.

If my talk is on stage presence, humor, or the need to use a variety of delivery techniques, I mention my experience as a comedic stage actor. I mention my time as a middle-aged groupie following the World Champions and studying with them if I'm talking about my growth as a speaker. Later, in the body of my speech, I show them where I was, where I am now, and how I got here.

4. Find ways to make your introduction set up something for your speech.

If I'm speaking to new presenters or nervous presenters, I include mention of my *Panic to Power* CD, which I co-created with three World Champions of Public Speaking. My panic moments were times, early in my speaking career, when I didn't know how to connect. The content of the CD sets up the content of my presentation.

5. Turn everything about you into everything for them.

"As a middle-aged groupie following world class speakers, Kathryn has picked up keys that have unlocked the doors of her speaking potential and helped her become a professional speaker. These keys are not easy to come by, but when you master them, your own speaking level will be raised to ..."

Next time you hear a speaker being introduced, take note: Was it all about the speaker and his or her irrelevant credentials and accomplishments, with no mention of how the audience may benefit? Or did the speaker, in writing the introduction, follow the five guidelines above and ignite the audience before ascending the platform?

Feel free to use humor in the introduction, as I do when I state, "Kathryn is a middle-aged groupie." That always evokes laughter. But more so, the use of humor helps you gage the energy level of the audience before you go to the platform.

I challenge you to work on your introductions. Making use of the five steps above will enthuse and energize your audience and make them eager to hear you. They will be connected to you *before you have even uttered a word of your message.*

TAKE YOUR AUDIENCE
ON A JOURNEY

"PEOPLE WON'T FOLLOW YOU
UNLESS THEY CAN SEE THE
PROMISE OF THE FUTURE."

–JIM ROHN,
SPEAKER AND AUTHOR

Has anyone ever invited you on a journey? What enticed you, engaged you, and intrigued you so much that you couldn't wait to get started?

PROMISE: A speech or presentation is similar to a journey, and you, the speaker, are the person inviting an audience to accompany you. If you want them to travel along with you to reach a more enlightened place, you must engage them immediately and keep them engaged throughout your talk; otherwise you'll end up journeying alone.

ROADMAP: Using the checklist below, pack your suitcase with just the essentials for a great speech: items that create a solid Structure, compelling Content, and a dynamic Delivery.

A CHECKLIST OF ESSENTIALS
FOR TAKING YOUR AUDIENCE
ON A JOURNEY

Before you start preparing your speech, ask yourself: Am I clear in what I want the audience to think, feel, say, or do differently after I finish speaking? Is my foundational phrase or takeaway message brief, concise, and doable?

Structure: HOW You Set It Up

Have you packed …

[ ] A strong opening for your speech that will hook them in and engage them right away, making it all about and for the audience?

[ ] A big promise about the benefits, rewards, or opportunities they'll receive by listening and adhering to your message?

[ ] A clear roadmap and destination for the audience?

[ ] Signposts and transitions throughout your speech to demonstrate good organization and an easy flow from one point to the next?

[ ] Times when you will touch base and connect, such as rhetorical reflective statements and questions?

[ ] A well-thought-out closing that states a clear, doable next step for your audience to take home with them?

Content: WHAT You Say

Have you packed …

[ ] A clear Foundational Phrase/takeaway message? Is it fewer than 10 words, you-focused, and easy to remember (a catchy, repeatable phrase)?

[ ] Anchors for your point(s)?

[ ] Reflection-type questions?

[ ] Techniques to achieve the results suggested?

[ ] A strong attempt to sell them your message by posing negative consequences if they don't buy into it and positive results if they do?

[ ] Stories, with characters/dialogue, instead of lists of facts?

[ ] The word "you" to stress you-focused messages?

[ ] Humor?

[ ] A tempting title that will make your audience curious about what you're going to impart (as opposed to a title that gives the message away)?

[ ] A memorable conclusion, using callbacks to previous points, characters, and events and a call to action stating the benefits?

The closing is your final opportunity to ask your audience to think differently or do something new. What was it you intended the audience to think feel, say, or do differently after you finished speaking?

Delivery: HOW You Say It

Are you aware of the need to pack some accessories and avoid others? Do pack:

[ ] Energy, initially matching the audience's level and then taking them to where you want them to go

[ ] Movement, planning your gestures and placement on the platform with purpose and ensuring congruency between body language and words

[ ] Variety, making sure you use pauses to avoid stepping on the audience's thoughts and laughs

Avoid packing:

- A sermon

- A monologue (talking *at* them as opposed to *with* them)

- A speaker man or speaker woman tone of voice

- General phrases of address like "How many of you …", "Who here …", "Does anyone …"

- A script that has you lip-synching with slides

Next time you speak, I challenge you to pack your suitcase with the essentials for an inspiring speech. Entice your audience to take that journey with you so they can return home more enlightened and hopeful.

Bon voyage, my fellow speaker.

THE KEYS OF A
KILLER KEYNOTE

"Before you inspire with emotion, you must be swamped with it yourself. Before you can move their tears, your own must flow. To convince them, you must yourself believe."

–Sir Winston Churchill

common aspiration of speakers is to be a keynote speaker at a conference. A welcome incentive to learning how to put one together is the great recognition a keynote entails, not to mention the handsome fee you can charge. Common questions speakers ask, though, are:

- How do you transform an idea into a full-length keynote speech?

- Where do you start?

PROMISE: The following gives you a modular approach to creating a keynote speech—a process for assembling the modules. It by no means gives you everything you need to know about keynote creations but does provide you with a solid skeletal framework for creating one. This knowledge will set you up with a starting point for assembling your own successful keynote speech.

ROADMAP: We'll look at the Keys of a Killer Keynote:

- What a keynote speech is

- The components of a keynote in terms of Structure, Content, and Delivery

What Is a Keynote Speech?

First, let's start with a definition of a keynote. Webster's dictionary says it is *"the first and harmonically fundamental tone of a scale."* In a speaking context, a keynote address is a speech that:

- Strikes the "key" note in a conference

- Can be anywhere from 30 minutes to an hour in length

- Promotes one central theme

- Motivates/inspires

The Components of a Keynote

Structure and Content

First and foremost, do you know what you want the audience to take away from your speech? What you want them to think feel say or do *differently* after you speak? Do you have a clear, concise foundational phrase?

The notes below relate not to the order of preparation but to the elements of your final masterpiece.

1. Opening (three parts)

BIG BANG

- Start with a you question, a story, a quotation, a profound statement, or any other way you choose to grab the audience's undivided attention.

- Get them committed and nodding their heads in agreement with you

BIG PROMISE

- Use the BOB Formula—Build On Benefits

- State benefits that hit all the letters of the EDGE sales formula (see above, page 22) to ensure your audience members will identify with at least one. Get to the benefits quickly so your audience will buy into wanting to listen and receive

- Make your promise irresistible—for example:

    - "In the next ___ minutes, you'll have the opportunity to pick up/discover …"

    - "For you, this means …"

- Give promises to others based on the expertise you have and want to share with them

A ROADMAP of where you're taking them

- Tell them where you're taking them (what they're going to hear)

- State either the number of steps; an acronym with each initial letter of the acronym representing a different point; all of your points upfront; or three or four letters without giving away the words they represent ("We'll be discussing the 4C's to Contentment")

2. **Body**

MODULES

Place each point in a separate module; each module is complete on its own and is composed of the PARTS Formula. That is, each one has a Foundational Phrase, Anchor, Reflection questions, Technique(s), and a Sale of the message or point. (See pages 18–21.)

People need to trust you. They don't care what you've won as long as you tell them where you've struggled and failed and the process of succeeding. Put the process you've learned, not yourself, on the pedestal. Reveal to them one or more of the Five F's—your Firsts, Flaws, Fears, Failures, and Frustrations—and how you resolved the issues you faced. Provide your audience with a message of hope.

ANCHORS

- After each point, anchor it with an anecdote, analogy, acronym, or activity so they will remember the point. Choose the best anchor to suit the point or message you've made. This ensures a variety of anchors throughout your keynote. Never make a point without an anchor

TRANSITIONS

Transitions are such important links between your modules or talking points that you can actually call them the glue that holds your entire speech together. Using a callback is a tactful way to allow the audience to review and relive the former point; then tease them as a way of taking them forward into the next point.

Two kinds of transitions can be used—what Craig Valentine calls a silver spoon transition or a verbal knife transition.

A silver spoon transition teases the audience into listening attentively because they will want to *attain* that next point. For example:

> *"If you get this next point, you will discover more hidden talents and strengths than you ever dreamed you had ... Imagine where your life could go when you ..."*

The verbal knife transition pushes the audience away from what they want to *avoid*. For example:

> *"If you simply practice speaking and never learn new tools and pick up new knowledge, you will be at a standstill as a wannabe speaker and never become world class. You will likely live in regret, saying: If only I had ... I wish I had ..."*

3. **Close**

The ultimate goal of a motivational speech is the *call to action*—a clear next step accompanied by a sense of urgency. After calling back, possibly to characters and events, and recapping your main points, close strong. You do this through your sincere, authentic emotions and your ability to speak with passion, compassion, and conviction. Your task is to inspire the audience and lift them up with hope and encouragement.

Whether you're giving a keynote or a shorter presentation, apply these same concepts regarding the Content, Structure, and Delivery to your speeches. The guidelines apply to every type of speech.

STYLE OF DELIVERY

What do pianists and keynote speakers have in common when it comes to their performances?

Great pianists:

- Demonstrate passion for the art of music by playing from the heart

- Not only maintain their audience's interest but move them emotionally and may even hold them spellbound

- Do this by striking many notes and varying their tempo and volume to create different moods

Similarly, great speakers:

- Speak from the heart (the secret here is to remain authentic to the person you are off stage; replicate who you are in your everyday life or you will be seen as fake, over-rehearsed, contrived, and definitely not conversational)

- Express many moods and emotions, creating an engaging symphony of melodic verbal communication for their listeners

- Strike many notes within a conversational tone that connects with many people. Sustaining the same tone or note throughout the entire speech would be flat, boring, and even irritating

A suggestion: If you plan to be a keynote speaker, I strongly advise you to keep:

- A life lesson or message file

- A story file

- An anchor file

- An activity file

You'll be grateful for these files when a keynote speech request comes your way because you won't have to start from a blank sheet.

LESSONS FOR NOT
LOSING YOUR AUDIENCE

"Perfect Prior Preparation Prevents Poor Performance."

–Peter Urs Bender,
Secrets of P-O-W-E-R Presentations

Losing an audience at any time of a presentation is a disaster for any speaker. Losing an audience due to lack of preparation is unforgivable.

> **PROMISE:** By spending time and effort in the preparation stage when you're crafting your next speech, you will avoid losing your audience and succeed in delivering a powerful presentation.

> **ROADMAP:** Looking at 10 Ways to Hold Your Audience will help you ensure that you always do!

10 WAYS TO HOLD YOUR AUDIENCE

1. Open strongly.

You need a strong opening that will hook your audience and make them want to listen attentively.

First, get their attention with a quotation, question, bold statement, story, or unusual action, while establishing a connection and inviting them in.

Second, use the word "you" as often as possible. Convince your audience that your message is worth hearing by stating the benefits they will receive from listening to you.

Third, give them a roadmap so they know where you'll be taking them.

2. Give them a tight structure.

What is loose is lost. The problem is that a confused, uninterested mind always says no.

Know your message and be able to say it in fewer than 10 words. Be precise and concise with it and your audience will opt in to listen and learn (as long as the message promises them life benefits, that is).

3. Address emotions.

Use personal stories to connect with your audience: (a) emotionally with your heart and (b) empathetically through your personal stories. All too often speakers state a quotation or a statistic to appeal to their audience's intellect, failing to show how the fact has impacted their own life.

Recall life lessons that you have learned. Anchor them to stories, recalling for your audience the associated sights, sounds, and sensations. *You've got life lessons to teach and the audience has life lessons to learn.*

4. Bring them inside your topic.

Bring your audience into your presentation by asking rhetorical, reflective questions. Use the most important word, *you*, in your questions and pause while they think. "Wisdom comes from reflection" (Patricia Fripp).

5. Talk *with* your audience.

Instead of talking *at* your audience by preaching and pontificating, talk *with* them in a personable, natural, sincere, conversational manner.

6. Welcome laughter.

Allowing your audience to laugh with you and even at you is a surefire recipe for … success. Let them have some fun at your expense; it shows that you can see the lighter side of life and yourself. When people laugh, they relax; when they relax, they learn; when they learn, they remember.

7. Give them hope.

If you never build *hope* into your presentation, you will leave your audience down or confused. Show them the possibilities and benefits of taking action in thought, feeling, word, and deed. You know how you leave a musical humming the tunes you've just heard? You want your audience to leave with your key message uppermost in their minds.

8. Make it all about them.

Don't make yourself the hero, rambling on with stories that are all about you and the great things you have done. You will be seen as an arrogant know-it-all. You will alienate your audience. Put the learning of the lesson, not you, on a pedestal. Make someone else, not you, the guru, the source of wisdom.

9. Give them less.

Squeezing too much information ends up in squeezing the

audience out. If you ramble and never get to the point, they will tune you out. Ensure that your content supports your key message. Less is more.

10. **Use fresh material.**

If you're going to use dated material, acknowledge that you're aware it's dated. Give value by bringing in something unique about what you're quoting.

I challenge you to reflect on which behaviors you have exercised in previous speeches and to take extra time in your preparation of upcoming speeches, working on one new initiative at a time.

As Peter Urs Bender has stated: "If you fail to prepare, you prepare to fail."

Move from Mediocre to Masterful

"Most people don't want to be most people. Whenever you use the phrase 'most people' you put a desire in your audience to not become one of those people; instead, they want to separate themselves from the 'most people' pack. Most speakers give speeches that get a good response, but masterful speakers give speeches that move their audience to action."

–Craig Valentine,
1999 World Champion of Public Speaking

W here do you want to be as a speaker? A mediocre type in the "most people" category or one of the stars in the "master speakers" category?

PROMISE: If you want to avoid being part of the "most people" category and want to rise above the rest as a speaker, you need to invest time and effort excelling not only in the structure and content of your speeches, but also in your delivery.

ROADMAP: To commit to being a master speaker, examine both columns below to determine which delivery techniques you already use or which ones you need to develop in order to reach the stars.

DON'T BE LIKE MEDIOCRE SPEAKERS

Avoid these 12 most common delivery mistakes:

1. Preaching, pontificating

2. Stepping on the audience's thoughts and laughs

3. Lip-synching with slides

4. Moving without purpose

5. Giving a monologue

6. Speaking to the entire group using words like: "How many of you ...?", "Has anyone ...?", "Who has ...?", "Everyone here is likely ..."

7. Being unnatural—speaking like another person (becoming speaker man or speaker woman)

8. Failing to match the audience's energy level

9. Staying at the same level for too long

10. Placing barriers between you and the audience

11. Never smiling—focusing too much on structure and content

12. Trying to be perfect by memorizing the speech

Do Be Like Master Speakers

You can be like master speakers by:

1. Talking with the audience in a conversational manner, avoiding the word "should"

2. When asking a question, pausing and letting them reflect on their inner voice. When they laugh, let them enjoy that time

3. If you choose to use PowerPoint, use less text, more graphics. A picture says a thousand words. Use the B button to darken the screen when you speak; this will help you avoid competing with your visuals. Remember, PowerPoint is an aid; you are the messenger

4. Moving mindfully, using the three reasons to move: illustrating time line, action, change of action

5. Your speech should be part of a two-way street between you and your audience.

6. Speaking to one, looking to all; use the "you" word in your content and look to all with your eyes

7. Being your natural yet enlarged self

8. Pacing and Leading; practice your speech by internalizing concepts and flow of speech as opposed to memorizing it

9. Varying your voice, gestures, and movement, because sameness is the enemy of the speaker

10. Removing anything between you and the audience: tables, lecterns, etc.

11. Smiling and making a connection before you say anything; having fun

12. Being personable and human; learning a speech so well that you internalize it

Whether you have to make few or many delivery changes in order to move from the mediocre speakers category to the Master Speakers' one, make small changes but do so often. Proceed one step at a time until you have mastered the techniques that bring you closer to your audience and make your speech memorable.

Nerves Are Natural
and Normal

"STAGE FRIGHT IS A
DECEPTIVE TERM. IT IMPLIES
THAT YOU WILL FEEL
NERVOUS THE MOMENT YOU
GET UP ON STAGE, WHEN
IN FACT YOU ARE NERVOUS
FROM THE MOMENT
YOU GET THE ASSIGNMENT."

–STEVE ALLEN,
COMEDIAN

"THERE ARE TWO KINDS
OF SPEAKERS: THOSE
THAT ARE NERVOUS AND
THOSE THAT ARE LIARS."

–MARK TWAIN

The degree of stage fright varies from person to person, and from situation to situation. It can range from nominal nervousness to paralyzing panic. Where are you, on a continuum from 1 to 10?

110

You may feel nervous or anxious when you're expected to introduce yourself to a group, address a staff meeting, or give a presentation. Did you know that even experienced speakers are nervous before they speak? Did you know that nervousness can be a good thing—that you can use it to your advantage?

>PROMISE: A degree of nervousness is good thing; it's a normal part of presenting. It tells you that what you're going to do is important to you. It reminds you to do your best. It gives you the extra rush of energy that can result in a more animated, passionate, and powerful delivery. Your nerves can be settled down, and your speaking elevated in quality and power, if you delve into and reflect on

the following discussion of nerves and how to deal with them.

ROADMAP: Let's look at the importance of understanding, recognizing, and accepting your nervous habits. It's also important to deal with your nerves if you're going to move ahead as a speaker.

UNDERSTANDING YOUR NERVOUSNESS

Most people feel nervous when speaking in front of an audience. Taken to the extreme, the prospect of speaking causes some people to avoid work or course assignments, or even presentations that are important to their career. If you're in this camp, you need to learn how to cope with your nervousness. Maybe you've earned a reputation as being knowledgeable and credible in a specific field and you want others to hear what you have to say, but your nervousness holds you back.

The good news is that you *can* do something about it. You *can* learn to be a confident, comfortable speaker.

Are you nervous because you think you'll make a mistake, forget a line, or lose your spot? You're human and therefore fallible. If you miss a line or two, no one's going to realize it—you're the only one who knows your script, so just carry on.

Right from the start, establish a rapport with your audience. Connect with them. Give them a valuable message and they will be endeared to you and will be forgiving if you happen to stumble occasionally. (The operative word here is "occasionally." An audience doesn't expect *perfection*, but they do need a speaker to be *personable and prepared*.)

RECOGNIZING YOUR NERVOUS HABITS

Are you aware of any nervous habits?

- Pacing on the platform

- Fidgeting with hands, hair, clothing

- Avoiding eye contact with audience

- Uttering many um's and ah's—filler words

• Speaking too slowly or too fast without any pauses

• Standing rooted to one spot, perhaps clinging to the lectern

• Experiencing butterflies

• Experiencing dry mouth, "jello" knees, racing heart

I sincerely hope what Craig Valentine has to say will ease your anxiety to a certain degree. He explains the 10X Phenomenon in *Panic to Power*, the CD I co-created with him and other World Champions of Public Speaking. Here's what he says:

> *"... What is happening inside of you is 10 times more amplified than what the audience actually perceives. They probably do not even notice that you are as nervous as you really are ... In a nutshell, the 10X phenomenon lets you know that you do not look 10% as bad as you feel."*

ACCEPTING YOUR NERVOUSNESS

Rather than spending time focusing on and trying to control or overcome your nerves, accept the fact that you are supposed to feel a degree of nervousness, since the success of your speech is important to you. Don't give attention and power to your nerves, because if you do, they will control you.

The Law of Attraction states that you draw to yourself whatever you focus on. In other words, what you focus on expands. So focus on positives. The five points below will help you change your mindset.

1. *Alter your mindset.* Turn your feeling of nervousness into a feeling of positive energy; use this energy to your advantage.

2. *Believe in and focus on your message.* You have a valuable message for others to hear; speak from your heart with conviction (the heart always wins over the head).

3. *Shift the spotlight from you to the audience.* Speaking is about them, not you. The audience needs to learn your lesson, so focus on and concern yourself with your purpose for them and the benefits they will receive.

4. *Connect with your audience.* You can do this by anchoring your points with your personal stories, your you-focused reflective questions, your authentic, sincere emotions, and your genuine concern for your audience.

5. *Understand that the audience wants you to succeed.* They are not your enemy. They don't want you to fail; that would be painful for them, too.

I encourage you to understand and recognize your nervousness. That said, don't focus on your nerves or try to control them; that will make them your chief concern and as a result they will control you.

10 Tips for Dealing with Your Nerves

1. *Believe in your message.* Choose a topic about which you're passionate. Be clear about the message you wish to impart and how it will benefit your audience. Feeling clear and confident about your message will make it much easier for you to relax. You will focus more on the message and its benefits for the audience rather than on yourself. *Speak from the heart and they will listen.*

2. *Prepare.* Put as much time and effort into the *delivery* of your speech as you do into the writing of your *content.* Know your material: practice, practice, practice. *Stand up while you practice* to ensure that your body language matches your words. Internalize the outline of your speech's main points and their sequential flow, as op-

posed to memorizing your speech word for word, which will make you more nervous.

3. *Memorize only the beginning and the ending of your speech.* This will help you feel more confident and secure at the start, when you're most nervous, and at the conclusion, when you need to focus on a strong call to action.

4. *Prepare mentally.* Visualize the outcome you want: a successful presentation. Remember the power of **positive thinking**.

5. *Smile.* When you smile, you feel happier and it makes you appear more relaxed. Remember, you rarely look as nervous on the outside as you feel on the inside. Smiling people appear more confident, comfortable, and in control. Smile and the audience will smile with you. Try it ... you'll like it.

6. *"Stage Time."* Get as much stage time as you can. Darren LaCroix states that there is no substitute for standing up and speaking in front of an audience as often as possible. The more you speak, the more comfortable you will become and the more effective you will become.

7. *Believe that the audience is fully supportive.* The audience is not your enemy. Keep in mind that if it is enjoyable for

you, it will be enjoyable for them, too. That's why they want you to succeed.

8. *Make eye contact.* Making eye contact creates a warm, inviting, friendly, conversational format. Remember, a speech is a conversation. You communicate verbally but also with your body. If you're fearful of making eye contact, deal with that specific fear right at the start. From the moment you walk up to the front, pause, connect with your eyes, and smile.

9. *Focus on your body.* Before speaking, breathe slow and deep. Focused breathing is what I'm talking about. Don't hyperventilate and pass out. Also, before you walk to the front, relax your shoulders and sit straight. Then walk confidently by standing tall, straightening your back, keeping your head up, and smiling. The position of your body can affect the way you feel.

10. *Remember to have fun.* If you do, so will your audience. Your audience will reflect whichever emotion you're demonstrating. They are your mirror.

Which of these tips have you possibly adopted in the past? If you're at the point where you feel you don't need these tips for dealing with your fear of speaking, share them with others who may benefit from knowing them.

The Little Engine That Could said: I think I can, I think I can, I think I can ...

Let's wrap up with a challenge for you to believe in yourself and your potential and affirm yourself. Say to yourself: I *know* I can, I *know* I can, I *know* I can ...

AND YOU WILL!

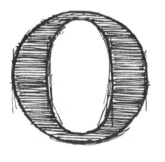

Outstanding Openings Rule Over Ordinary Ones

"RESEARCH SHOWS THAT WE START TO MAKE UP OUR MINDS ABOUT OTHER PEOPLE WITHIN SEVEN SECONDS OF FIRST MEETING THEM ... WE ARE COMMUNICATING WITH OUR EYES, FACES, BODIES, AND ATTITUDES ... CONSCIOUSLY OR UNCONSCIOUSLY, WE'RE SIGNALING TO OTHER PEOPLE WHAT OUR TRUE FEELINGS ARE AND WHAT WE WANT TO HAPPEN IN OUR ENCOUNTER."

–ROGER AILES,
YOU ARE THE MESSAGE

F irst impressions are lasting impressions. How we open our speeches is therefore crucial. We must place immense importance on always opening strong.

PROMISE: By understanding and utilizing the law of primacy (what the audience hears first), you will instinctively structure the opening of your presentation with a big bang that will get your audience interested, committed, and nodding their heads in agreement with you.

ROADMAP: We'll discuss five ways to take charge of the stage at the outset of your speech. The first four ways deal with content, and the last one with manner of delivery. The five ways are: rhetorical question, original or interesting story, powerful quotation, interesting statistic or known fact, and the manner of delivery.

As a speaker, you, like me, have likely agonized over speech openings, thinking: "Which is the best way to begin? Which way is the most effective and powerful? Which way will have most impact on my audience and make me more memorable?"

There is no one way to start. However, whichever way you choose, start with the end in mind—with your takeaway message in mind. What do you want the audience to think, feel, say, or do differently *after* you speak?

Connect the opening of your speech to the close of your speech—your takeaway message Your presentation's first 30 seconds (primacy) and last 30 seconds (recency) must be the strongest and most powerful parts of your speech, since they are what the audience will remember most.

FIVE WAYS TO TAKE CHARGE OF THE STAGE

1. Ask a Rhetorical Question

"You" is the most powerful word in a speech. It brings the audience to you. It taps into the audience's own life experiences and gets them thinking and engaged. By connecting with them and inviting them in, you will make them want to journey with you. Focus on them *before* you get into the body of your presentation. Remember, it's all about *them* ... *not you.* Use the following types of questions:

"Have you ever ...?"

"What degree of fear did you feel when …?"

"When was the last time you …?"

"If you are a parent, were you aware that …?"

"Who, in your life, was so influential that …?"

These types of questions get an audience's attention by instilling curiosity, interest, and excitement in them.

2. Tell an Interesting Original Story

You may be familiar with speaker Bill Gove's expression: "Tell a story, make a point." Or you may have heard these words: "Facts tell, stories sell."

A well-crafted, well-told personal story that conveys the underlying message of your speech is an excellent way to begin a presentation. It:

- Establishes your credibility instantly

- Captures your audience's attention

- Connects you with your audience

Connection results when the audience, after listening to a vignette from your own life in which you faced some adversity and learned a process that helped you overcome it, views you as similar to them. Such stories trigger the universal emotions of happiness, sadness, surprise, disgust, fear, or anger. People are moved by emotions. We all experience the same emotions though we have different stories.

Personal stories also help you speak in a natural, conversational manner.

Mark Brown, 1995 World Champion of Public Speaking, says: "Nobody but you can tell your story, and nobody can tell your story the way you can."

Create a story file and store it for reference. Add to it as new stories arise.

A word of warning: Avoid boasting about yourself, appearing superior, or placing yourself on a pedestal; these actions will alienate you from your audience.

3. Use a Powerful Quotation

If you choose to use a quotation, use one that proves or supports your message. Try to avoid trotting out an overused or well-known one. Consider what you think when you hear one of these quotations: "Oh no, not that one again."

Remember to keep your opening interesting, unique, and fresh for your audience, so they will be interested and intrigued. Consider using a quotation made by a family member, a boss, or a friend. Or use one you have heard repeatedly, one that has taught you a life lesson that you want to share with others. A quotation is also a great tool to tie your presentation together and give you direction.

Be sure to relate the meaning and importance of the quotation to your life and how it can also bear on the audience's lives.

Another word of warning: Remember to give the source and the exact wording of the quote. If you cannot remember either of the above, do not use it because if you do, you will definitely lose credibility with your audience.

4. Cite an Interesting Statistic

If you decide to open with a fact or interesting statistic, make it you-focused right from the start. For example:

"It may interest you to know that according to ..."

"You may have thought that … but what this survey states is …"

"Did you realize that Gallup has discovered that …?"

Remember, people are not moved by facts; they are moved by emotions. Discuss how the statistic has been or could be relevant to both your life and possibly to theirs. You may use the facts of the statistic in a personal story so the message will be emotionally connected and solidly anchored.

Your audience needs to hear and feel whatever feeling you experienced, the process you learned, how you learned it, and most importantly, how they can achieve a similar outcome.

5. **Watch You Manner of Delivery**

Speakers often start off at an energy level that does not match the audience's. This is a surefire way to lose an audience.

You can assess the audience's energy level by watching them during other speakers' sessions or while you're being introduced. Check their energy level, match it, and then, and only then, take them where you want them to go. Depending on your goals and objectives, if it is low, match it, then build it up, and if it is high, match it and then take it down. This is what Craig Valentine calls "Pace and Lead."

I encourage you to be creative in opening your presentations. Speaking is about connection, and connection must be established at the outset of your presentation. Good luck in creating lasting impressions.

MIND YOUR P'S—PAUSES

"THE RIGHT WORD MAY BE
EFFECTIVE, BUT NO WORD
WAS EVER AS EFFECTIVE AS A
RIGHTLY TIMED PAUSE."

–MARK TWAIN

There's a simple but powerful way for you to enhance your audience's wisdom: by using pauses so they can reflect on your message and hear their own inner voice.

PROMISE: If you use appropriately timed pauses, you will be regarded as a powerful presenter who creates positive change. Why do pauses create change? Because change starts in your listeners' thoughts and pauses allow them to … think. The inner dialogue or thoughts that occur in their minds are what truly effective presentations are all about.

ROADMAP: We will examine the incredible cause-and-effect relationship between pauses and quietness, exploring how the pause is the technique and silence is the message.

Many speakers think speaking is a monologue—a one-way conversation. The speaker speaks and the listener listens. But this type of presentation is more like a lecture. Speakers, especially new ones, often race through a speech because they lack the courage to pause. Their discomfort is quite normal. However, avoiding pauses doesn't work.

Audiences tune out when they hear constant talking. They simply can't keep up.

On the other hand, audiences also zone out when a speaker plods through a presentation.

Some speakers do use pauses but time them inappropriately or just drop them in at random, confusing their audience. Often these are speakers who have been advised to add more pauses but don't know when, why, or for how long.

A word of warning: If you're just going to pause to look poised, then you're simply feeding your ego. It's contrived, unnatural, and fake, and it results in confusing and losing the audience. Dramatic pauses produce a negative effect.

So *when* does one pause? Just as an action word prompts purposeful movement on the platform, so a powerful statement or question should prompt a reflecting pause.

And *why* does one pause? A presentation is all about the thoughts in the minds of the audience. That said, when a speaker places reflective pauses at appropriate times in a speech, the silence created can say much more than the words. A powerful presentation is really a dialogue between the speaker and the audience, and even more so it's a dialogue that occurs in the little voice within the listener's head.

A powerful presenter knows when and why to pause so the audience can reflect on the point or message in silence.

Speakers not only need to offer new thoughts to an audience, they also need to give them time to think. True change occurs with the thoughts of the listener. That means we must place our pauses at times when we want the audience to reflect. It would be a good strategy for you to time your pauses in connection with your you-focused questions or statements. For example:

> *"What caused you to make that personal decision to stay?"*
> *PAUSE.*

Pause before and after important ideas. This lets the idea or statement sink into the minds and hearts of your audience. It allows them to fully digest what you have said before you move on to your next point. Comedians create humor and laughter by following this structure:

Set-up

Pause

Punch-line

Pause

This structure causes the audience to laugh and allows them to laugh—because the pause keeps the comedian from stepping on the audience's laugh time. (This is why comedians say humor is all about timing.)

Speakers need to do the same by structuring a word sequence that places their power words (the words that carry the meaning of the sentence or phrase) at the end—before a pause.

The length of the pause should be based on the importance of the power word.

- A short powerful phrase saturated with meaning may need repetition and then a pause. Pausing alone in this case may not suffice. Mindful repetition gives an additional moment for the audience to really absorb what you're saying. Overdoing this, however, will irritate them

- A simple yes or no question requires only a brief pause

- If we ask our audiences to reflect deeper into their memories, we must give them more time to go there and reflect. If we don't, we are truly not there for them

If you still have difficulty with initiating pauses, try counting three "heart beats" after asking reflective questions. This will give you something to do while you're not talking. Using effective pauses and living with the resulting silence does eventually get easier.

Remember the importance of people needing to hear their inner voice when they are given time to reflect. Their refection on an important point creates an opportunity for them to change and grow.

MIND YOUR Q'S—
QUOTATIONS AND
QUESTIONS

"SINCE WISDOM COMES FROM
REFLECTION, PEOPLE NEED
TO HEAR NOT ONLY
YOUR VOICE BUT THEIR
INNER VOICE THAT COMES
FROM REFLECTION."

–Patricia Fripp, CSP, CPAE,
SPEAKER AND AUTHOR

U sed well, quotations and questions make a quantitative and qualitative difference.

Using quotations as references can be effective, but only if the speaker knows when, why, and how to use them appropriately and poignantly.

> **PROMISE:** You can use well-chosen quotations and reflective questions followed by quietness to enhance your message greatly and set yourself apart from other speakers.

> **ROADMAP:** First we'll see how quotations and questions are used ineffectively. Then we'll see when, why, and how to use them to make a qualitative and quantitative difference in how you connect with your audience.

USING QUOTATIONS

Quotations are used *ineffectively* when they are:

- Overused with no new twist to their interpretation

- Not personalized—when their meaning and significance are not linked to you and your message

- Not quoted accurately

- Not credited clearly to their creators

- Too numerous for one speech

- Too long

To be powerful and meaningful, quotations must be used judiciously. They should be brief and be deployed sparingly. For credibility with your audience, quote people whose work you know well. This strengthens the trust the audience has in you as a speaker and an authority on your topic.

A well-chosen quotation can serve many purposes. It can:

- Be a strong anchor by reinforcing a previous point

- Serve very effectively in the opening or closing of a speech

If a quotation is used to support a point, make sure it doesn't overtake the point but solidly and strongly supports it.

Also, be sure to relate to the audience the significance of the quotation to your own life. The audience's interest lies in finding out about what meaning the quotation has for you and how it has helped better your life. The audience wants to know your message and what you have to say. If you happen to use an overused quotation, acknowledge that fact openly but add a new twist to it and its meaning for you.

USING QUESTIONS

Questions are used *ineffectively* when they are:

- Not you-focused

- Not followed by an appropriate pause

- Too long and confusing for the listeners

- Not related to the previous or following point

- Used too often with no acknowledgment of the results (saying, "Raise your hands if …" and then not commenting)

Questions asked at different times of your speech are extremely effective for communicating, being conversational, and connecting. Most importantly, though, if followed by an appropriately timed pause, they provide possible life-changing opportunities for the listeners. Why? Because listeners can reflect on their own situations and then can choose to change and grow.

Remember, a presentation is all about the listeners' thoughts, their processing of those thoughts, and their decisions to possibly change and better their lives.

Think again about using the PARTS Formula (see pages 18–21) to create compelling content. Make a conscious effort to ask rhetorical questions to get your audience to think about their own situation as it relates to a point you made. Try to come up with a bold statement you can make about this point and then embed it in a scenario, real or hypothetical, so the audience can actually visualize themselves there with an important decision to make.

The best reflection questions are open-ended: Who, What, When, Where, Why questions. For example:

"When was the last time you ...?"

"Who was the person who influenced you to ...?"

"What was it that ...?"

"Where were you when ...?"

"Why did you decide to ...?"

You could also try another format of questioning: asking for a show of hands. Once again, make sure your request is you-focused. Do *not* ask the question in this manner: "How many of you ...?" When you address or talk to all, you in fact talk to no one.

Ask it this way: "Raise your hand if ..." In this case, you're actually speaking and connecting to one in content by using the word "your," yet you're looking to all with your eyes.

When you do ask for a show of hands, scan the number of raised hands, react, and address the small or large number. "Oh, so few of you seem to ..." or "Wow, what a great number of you ..." It is important for the audience to note that the activity had some value and was done for a reason.

One last suggestion about questions. If you plan to have a Q&A session, place it *within* your presentation, not at the very end. Craig Valentine often tells a humorous story about how he learned this lesson. In a Q&A after he gave a talk, a woman asked him, "Mr. Valentine, do you think I could apply all this to *horses?*" Because his time was almost up, he had little chance to wrap up the way he wanted so that the message of his speech, rather than this bizzare question, would be what the audience took away with them.

A final thought on the last two chapters: If you mind your P's and Q's during your presentations, you will skillfully drive your points home, not only intellectually but also emotionally. The result? Your audience will remember your points and you. Why? Because your structure, content, and delivery techniques are world class.

ROCKIN' RACONTEURS
ARE REMEMBERED
AND REPEATED

" 'THOU SHALT NOT'
IS SOON FORGOTTEN, BUT
'ONCE UPON A TIME'
WILL LAST FOREVER."

–PHILIP PULLMAN,
SPEAKER AND AUTHOR

"SPEAKING IS SIMPLY:
TELL A STORY, MAKE A POINT;
TELL ANOTHER STORY,
MAKE ANOTHER POINT."

–BILL GOVE, CSP, CPAE,
AWARD-WINNING SPEAKER

The definition of a raconteur in Webster's dictionary is "a person skilled at telling stories."

What is it that rockin' raconteurs do so well that their stories are remembered and repeated?

PROMISE: You can rock as a raconteur and be strides ahead of other speakers by being aware of the elements that cause stories to be remembered and repeated.

ROADMAP: The R words that will be discussed are ones that rockin' raconteurs are conscious of as they plan and deliver their stories. These words are organized under the topics of Planning Stage, Stories, and Delivery. The words are:

- Result

- Rapport and Relate

- Reveal a Resolution

- Relive and Recapture

- Reflect and Realize

PLANNING STAGE

Start with the intended **result** or **end** in mind.

The most important question you need to ask yourself as you craft your speech or presentation is: "What is it I want my audience to think, feel, say, or do differently *after* I finish speaking? What is my takeaway message? Which stories would be most effective to evoke within an audience at least one of the six universal emotions—happiness, sadness, anger, surprise, disgust, and fear?"

As author, poet, and storyteller Deena Metzger puts it, "When stories are nestled in the body, soul comes forth."

STORIES

Storytelling creates an excellent, natural, conversational way to build **rapport** with and **relate** to your audience. A well-crafted story that **relates** to the audience's emotions and needs establishes your credibility instantly, captures the audience's attention, and creates immediate **rapport**.

Once you've established your similarities to your audience—that it's all about *them*, not you, and that they will benefit from listening and learning—you will create an emotional connection. Consequently, they will trust you and want to journey with you.

As story seminar facilitator and author Robert McKee says, "Stories are the creative conversion of life itself into a more powerful, clearer, more meaningful experience. They are the currency of human contact."

In your stories, **reveal a resolution** regarding an obstacle, issue, hardship you were able to overcome because of a process you previously learned.

Highlight the personal conflict in your stories, then **reveal a resolution** and a life lesson learned. We all have stories in which we've learned a process enabling us to think, feel, talk, or act differently, in a more enlightened way. Share these processes with others. They want to learn *what* you've learned and *how* you've learned it. Place the *process* (what you've learned), not the person (yourself), on a pedestal (Craig Valentine).

The poet (and doctor) William Carlos Williams once said, "Their story, yours and mine—it's what we all carry with us on this trip we take, and we owe it to each other to respect our stories and learn from them."

DELIVERY

Relive and recapture the sights, sounds, and sensations of your life stories.

Instead of telling your entire story in narrative form, ***relive and recapture*** scenes, just as you do with friends, by using characters, body language, and actual dialogue, including your own inner dialogue or thoughts. Captivate your audience by drawing them right into the movie of your story, helping them to view and hear it.

"People will remember what they heard, when they saw it!" –Patricia Fripp

"If you tell me, it's an essay. If you show me, it's a story." –Barbara Greene

"Don't retell a story; relive it!" –Lou Heckler

"Don't say the old lady screamed—bring her on and let her scream." –Mark Twain

As you deliver your stories, give the audience opportunities to **reflect** on your revelation/point/message so they **realize** that they, too, can achieve the same success in their lives.

At the beginning, in the middle, and at the end, continually engage your audience with *you* questions or statements. For example:

"Have you ever ...?"

"It may interest you to know ..."

"You have everything within you to ..."

"Do you realize that when you ... then you will be rewarded with ...?"

As speaker and author Roger C. Shank puts it, in "Tell Me a Story": "In the end all we have are stories and methods of finding and using those stories."

I challenge you to first realize the importance of using stories in order to connect.

Next, create and continually update a *story file* of your own life stories when you learned a life lesson.

Finally, be conscious of and use the R elements of Rockin' Raconteurs in the planning of the content and delivery of your stories.

Be a collector of stories and become a Rockin' Raconteur so your message can be **remembered** and **repeated**.

Rockin' Raconteurs are ***remembered*** and ***repeated*** because they know that:

- Stories are crucial for connecting emotionally with their audiences

- The point/message must be anchored in their stories in a fully present, heartfelt manner

- People are moved to action by emotion first, not intellect

- The R factors are crucial in the planning and delivery of their stories

- Everyone, regardless of age, gender, race, or creed, enjoys hearing stories and everyone learns from stories

STORIES SELL, WHILE
FACTS ONLY TELL

"FACTS ARE FREE,
STORIES ARE VALUABLE."

–DANIEL PINK,
A WHOLE NEW MIND

"STORY IS THE SINGLE MOST
POWERFUL WEAPON IN
A LEADER'S ARSENAL."

–HOWARD GARDNER
EDUCATION SPECIALIST AND AUTHOR

"STORYTELLING IS
THE MOST POWERFUL WAY
TO PUT IDEAS INTO
THE WORLD TODAY."

–ROBERT MCKEE,
HOLLYWOOD SCREENWRITER

Imagine this: You're at a business meeting. The lights are dimmed, the laptop and projector are turned on, and you're expected to sit through slide after slide after slide of data, facts, and figures. Are you still awake and enthused? Are you learning anything?

PROMISE: I invite you to visit Doug Stevenson's website www.storytelling-in-business.com and watch his video in the Media Gallery, "Storytelling in Business Is Serious Business." I know that as a result you'll view storytelling as a very powerful form of communication and you'll want to use it in your presentations ... even if you speak to groups in the corporate world.

ROADMAP: We'll examine why *facts tell and stories sell* by contrasting fact-based and story-based presentations.

When I was an educator and education consultant, I often heard other educators say: "But I taught it! Why didn't they learn it?" Does this question also relate to presenters? I believe it does. Just because a presenter says something, it doesn't mean the audience will relate to it, reflect on it, or remember it.

Can an audience be persuaded, motivated, and inspired to change their thoughts, feelings, words, and actions by being inundated with facts and figures? Or is an audience persuaded, motivated, and inspired by being engaged, involved, and connected on an emotional level through stories from a speaker's life experience?

Fact-based Versus Story-based Presentations

In what follows, notice the differences in the characteristics and effects of fact-based and story-based presentations. How would each style affect your audience?

In Fact-Based Presentations:

CONTENT

- Is composed of data, facts, information

- Is left-brain driven

- Is linear, content/intellect focused

SPEAKER

- Speaks more from the head

- Is caught up in memorizing facts and figures or relying on PowerPoint slides for info

DELIVERY

- Is usually lecture format ("talking at")

- Is static; speaker tends to remain in one spot or at speak and move at one pace with no purpose

- Is non-expressive; body language and voice tend to be within a narrow range ("Sameness is the enemy of the speaker," says Patricia Fripp)

AUDIENCE

- Tends to become bored, overloaded with data; may become zoned out

- Is not likely to be moved to action by the intellect

- Is not likely to be engaged

In Story-based Presentations:

CONTENT

- Is composed of stories combined with a variety of anchors for the main points

- Is right- and left-brain driven

- Is more creative and emotion focused, with a degree of focus on the intellect

SPEAKER

- Speaks from both the heart and the head

- Is fully present and in the moment by reliving scenes/events within stories, being conversational, touching base with audience

DELIVERY

- Is more conversational ("talking with")

- Allows for creation of scenes, characters, and purposeful movement .

- Speaker's body language and voice vary naturally through scenes, characters, dialogue ... speaker steps in and out of stories

AUDIENCE

- Tends to be more interested because this format is easier to follow and more enjoyable for them

- Is moved to action by emotion

- Is engaged and ready to change

So let me ask you: Are you more convinced now that *stories sell and facts only tell*?

TRANSITIONS—THE MOST NEGLECTED PARTS OF A SPEECH

"THE MOST NEGLECTED
PART OF A SPEECH IS THE
TRANSITION BETWEEN
ONE POINT AND THE NEXT."

–CRAIG VALENTINE,
1999 WORLD CHAMPION OF PUBLIC SPEAKING

W hy is there such excitement on rollercoaster rides? Because although the riders can see the coming turns, they are still sharp and exciting.

PROMISE: If you pay more attention to the turns, or transitions, in your presentations, making them sharp and exciting, you will have your audience at the edge of their seats, excited, enthused, and eager to hear more.

ROADMAP: We'll take a look at how to clearly and effectively break a previous pattern of a speech and alert the audience that they are transitioning to a slightly different but related theme, while maintaining their interest and curiosity.

Transitions—the spaces between points, the segues from one point to the next—are the most neglected parts of a speech. So often speakers move from one point to the next, assuming not only that the audience wants to move on, but also that they are actually still with them. Speakers may take all this for granted by saying such things as:

"My next point is ..."

"Point #3 is ..."

"Let's move on to the next step of ..."

As speakers it's our job to make the audience want to go on with us, by teasing them and enticing them to want to hear more. A speech flows when the transitions are smooth, tying all of the points together to a central theme.

Here is an example of how to entice them to want to hear more. Let's assume a speaker is discussing two major C points: **to commit to adopting a positive attitude** (a necessary preliminary mental action) and **to exercise courage to explore and try new things** (a physical action). The two points could be connected in a transition by purposely weaving in three factors:

- Where they've been with you in the speech

- Where you're taking them

- Why it's important for them to go there with you

To be more specific, in each transition:

1. *Remind* the audience where they have been (return to the first point about a Positive Attitude).

> *"After comparing the devastating effects of holding onto a negative attitude and the victorious effects of committing to and maintaining a positive attitude, it is obvious why winners have positive attitudes."*

> **Transition**: *"Now I ask you, what good is adopting the first C, a **commitment** to a positive mental attitude, if ..."*

2. *Show* them where they are going (state the next point by connecting it to the previous sentence).

> *" ... you lack the second C? In this case, this C involves physical action: exploring and trying new things. Let me ask you this. Have you ever experienced being fearful of doing something for the first time, but you did it and you not only survived but were successful? What held you back? What C trait do you think you were lacking? ... Yes, **courage**."*

3. *Tell them why* it's important for them to come along with you. Perhaps by telling a personal story, build on the

benefits for them—exactly what they will get by coming with you.

"Let me take you back seven years to when a friend helped me discover the wonderful benefits of great joy and self-fulfillment. These benefits are ones anyone can enjoy by exercising **courage** *to explore and try new things—in spite of the fear they may be experiencing. If you were with me in July 2003, you would have ..."*

A few reminders regarding transitions to ease the audience's journey in bridging from one point to the next:

- Memorize your transitions (highlight the entire transition paragraph in your script)

- Use you-focused questions and state benefits for the audience

- Tell a story/vignette

- Change stage locations, connecting a physical transition to your verbal transition (congruency between actions and words)

- Treat transitions, at times, as good opportunities for use of humor

My challenge to you is to be more aware of this most neglected part of speeches. The next time you work on a speech or presentation, breathe new life into it by paying close attention to your transitions. Your audience not only will stick with you, but they will also be excited about the next turn on the rollercoaster, or, in a gentler speech, pleased by how you ease them across the bridge to your next point.

UNIVERSAL
EMOTIONS UNITE

"EMOTION *IS* THE FAST LANE
TO THE BRAIN."

–DOUG STEVENSON,
SPEAKER AND AUTHOR

Do you know what the six universal emotions are? They are:

- Happiness

- Sadness

- Surprise

- Anger

- Disgust

- Fear

These emotions are experienced by every human being at one time or another.

> **PROMISE:** Speakers who tell a story exemplifying one of these emotions are bound to connect with their audience. People will recall experiencing a similar emotion, albeit as part of their own different story. When we realize that we need to stop

giving speeches and start having conversations, incorporating these universal emotions into our stories as we do with friends, we will be able to create a deep bond with our audiences.

ROADMAP: Let's look at why, where and when, and how we can use these universal emotions in our presentations.

WHY EMOTIONS ARE EFFECTIVE CONNECTORS

People are not moved to action through their intellect but through their emotions. Although we all have different life stories, we all experience the universal emotions at one time or another. Individuals in your audience will be able to connect and relate to your chosen emotion while recalling their own unique event. If one of your stories is significant and meaningful to you, it could very well be significant to others, too.

WHERE AND WHEN TO USE EMOTIONS

These slice-of-life stories can be told whenever a point needs to be anchored or emphasized. They do not need to be overly powerful Mount Everest stories (because very few people will be able to relate). Rather, they can be simple, everyday stories that embed a deep-seated, meaningful message or point.

HOW TO USE EMOTIONS IN YOUR SPEECH

The story is a speaker's greatest tool. A single story can be used to make a variety of points, depending on which points are appropriate for the situation.

Start by recalling personal stories from your past—recall their sights, sounds, and sensations. Whenever a story entertains, inspires, influences, or teaches you in any way, write it down. If a story had a significant impact on your life, it may very well have an impact on others. Record the stories, attaching a point to each one. Never use a story in a speech without making a point. If you have a story and no point for it, ask others to help you find one.

Here are **three important questions** you need to ask yourself in the pre-writing and writing stages of your speech:

1. What do I want my audience to think, feel, say, or do differently *after* I finish speaking? (What is the lesson they will learn that will enhance their life?)

2. Which personal story/stories should I use to best emphasize my message/point? Which stories demonstrate one of the six universal emotions?

3. Are my stories you-focused? Note that while the story may be about your experience, the message is *for them*. It's not told for you the speaker, but for *you the audience*. Check the number of times the words "I" and "you" occur on the pages of your script. There should be far more of the latter than the former.

If you haven't started a story file, this is a good time to do so. Add to it as time goes by and stories occur in your life. Then you'll find yourself with an abundance of life-enhancing lessons from which your listeners can learn.

Vocal Variety Brings Your Delivery to Life

"IT'S NOT ALWAYS WHAT
YOU KNOW THAT MATTERS,
IT'S HOW YOU PRESENT
IT ... THE POWER YOUR
VOICE COMMANDS IS VERY
IMPORTANT. IT'S EXTREMELY
CRITICAL IN ANY SITUATION
IN WHICH YOU HAVE TO
MAKE POINTS COME ACROSS.
IT DOES NOT MATTER WHO
YOU ARE, BELIEVABILITY
IS ONE OF YOUR MOST
IMPORTANT ASSETS."

–PETER URS BENDER,
SPEAKER AND AUTHOR

Your voice is a powerful tool. Are you using it to its full potential? I suggest you consider the art of speaking as the transformation of a one-dimensional text into a 3D experience. In other words, the way you use your voice is critical to making your content come *alive*.

PROMISE: Vocal variety has the power to establish credibility and an emotional connection with the audience. This connection is imperative, since a speaker's main purpose is to persuade, inspire, and influence the audience to reach greater heights.

ROADMAP: Vocal variety is created when you show *how* you feel about *what* you are saying. The key word here is "variety." Let's look at:

• Why varying your voice is so important

• The Four P's of vocal variety

• A few techniques for avoiding sameness in voice ("Sameness," as Patricia Fripp puts it, "is the enemy of the speaker")

Why Vocal Variety Is So Important

- Demonstrates passion, confidence, and conviction on the part of the speaker

- Captures the interest and attention of the audience

- Evokes emotion from the speaker, creating a connection with audience members

- Emphasizes certain points, words, phrases so the audience remembers

The Four P's of Vocal Variety

If you want your audience to experience a rollercoaster ride of emotions, vocal variety is the ticket. (The following is adapted from a graphic Peter Urs Bender created.)

Voice Qualities	Establishes Low Believability	Establishes High Believability
Projection (volume and tone)	Low	Contrast (varied)
Pitch (high/low)	High	Contrast (varied)
Pace (speed/rate)	Fast	
Pauses (breaks of silence in speeches)	Never	Used purposely at appropriate times

Emphasis is the stress given to words, points, or phrases to make them stand out and send the audience away remembering your main point or message.

A pause before emphasizing a word, point, or phrase is very effective, especially when followed by a change in pace, pitch, and projection. Whichever way you choose to emphasize a point, create a change in your voice. If you don't, the audience will not be able to sort out what's especially important.

The power of the pause is often overlooked, yet it is a profoundly effective tool in delivering a believable and memorable message. Pausing at the right moment in a speech can add emphasis to important points and make a lasting impression on the listener.

Before saying something important ... **pause** ... and after saying something important ... **pause**. The pause is the technique; the silence is the message, since "wisdom comes from reflection" (Patricia Fripp).

Audience members need time to reflect and realize the relevance of an important point made so they can apply it to their own lives.

A pause allows the audience to:

- Anticipate a big moment in the speech

- Make the transition from one point to the next

- Reflect on and react to a point ... hopefully reaching an *aha* moment

TECHNIQUES FOR LEARNING TO SPEAK NATURALLY WITH VOCAL VARIETY

- *Videotaping*: There is no better way to hear what you sound like when you're speaking to others than to record yourself. This will allow you to analyze your delivery and see which areas require improvement

- *Children's books*: If you tend to speak in a monotone, practice by reading children's stories aloud. You will automatically give the characters their own unique voices and you'll see and hear what your voice is capable of doing. Then take this ability with you the next time you speak, but remember not to perform with a contrived, rehearsed voice; be an enlarged but ***natural*** self

- Practice stepping into a story with characters and dialogue and then stepping out to pause before you stress an important point

- Listen to both good and bad speakers and note their use of voice. You can learn from hearing those who don't use their voice effectively and those who use it to maximize the audience's attention and interest in their speech

- Does your own voice enhance your content, making it come alive?

Words of Wisdom from
World Class Speakers

"Did you know 80% of paid speeches come from referral? That's why the number one marketing tool is being great on the platform."

–Speaking Secrets of the Champions (CD)

Craig
Valentine

Darren
LaCroix

Doug
Stevenson

Ed
Tate

Mark
Brown

Patricia
Fripp

The **words of wisdom** below exemplify all of these world class speakers when they stand and deliver from the platform. Analyze, understand, and absorb these sayings. Then see how you can use them in your own presentations, so you can enter the realm of world class speakers.

"The enemy of the speaker is sameness."

"Invite the audience into our mind."

"Create holograms on the platform."

"Make yourself similar, not special."

"Take them, don't just tell them!"

"Create a scene and commit to it."

"Share your 5 F's: your Firsts, Failures, Flaws, Fears, and Frustrations."

"Put the process, not the person, on a pedestal."

"Humor is uncovered, not added!"

"The heart of a presentation is a story; the heart of a story is dialogue."

"What is loose is lost; what is tight stays in sight; the phrase determines what stays."

"Emotion is the fast lane to the brain."

"Wisdom comes from reflection."

"A speech is not a monologue."

"Speak to one, look to all!"

"Go narrow and deep with your topic."

"Practice the laws of primacy, frequency, and recency for better retention of message."

"Don't just re-tell the story, re-live it!"

"Don't make yourself special, make yourself similar."

"Don't just take the stage, own it!"

"Stage time, stage time, stage time."

"Don't get ready, stay ready!"

"State a phrase that pays!"

"Push them into the Pull."

There are lots more words of wisdom that you, as a speaker, can work from to enhance your own speaking. Concentrate on doing whatever it takes to go from **good** to **great** on the platform. And if you remember just one thing from this chapter, let it be this:

"Don't speak for standing ovations; speak for standing invitations."

X Marks the Spot—
Moving with Purpose

"WHEN YOU SPEAK,
CREATE A SCENE
AND COMMIT TO IT."

–CRAIG VALENTINE,
1999 WORLD CHAMPION OF PUBLIC SPEAKING

"CREATE HOLOGRAMS
ON THE STAGE."

–DARREN LACROIX,
2001 WORLD CHAMPION OF PUBLIC SPEAKING

Have you ever watched a speaker who appears to be glued to one spot on the platform? Or, in contrast, have you ever watched a speaker who paces non-stop, practically giving you whiplash?

> **PROMISE:** Speaking involves both content and delivery. It transforms a one-dimensional text into a three-dimensional experience. Speaking is not simply *telling* the audience; it's also about *taking them* (getting them to use all their senses so they truly experience your stories and message). So doesn't it make sense, since you've spent much time preparing the content of your presentation, to spend time working out the delivery, by choreographing your script on the platform? Appropriate and timely movement during your speech will help make you and your message memorable.

> **ROADMAP:** Keeping in mind the expression "phrasing helps with staging," we will examine three main reasons to move mindfully, or purposefully, on the platform.

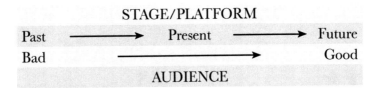

Phrasing Helps with Staging

There are three main reasons to move mindfully on the platform.

1. *To establish alignment between words and actions, and words and state.* This alignment gives you a valid reason to move.

   (a) Demonstrate traveling/action words.

   "I walked to my car and ..."

   "I saw the chair across the room and collapsed."

   "I boldly took a few steps forward."

   (b) Differentiate between opposites.

   You may want to differentiate between bad and good, negative and positive, or a problem and a solution. Use the audience's left side for the bad/ the negative/the problem, and their right side for the opposite, the good/positive/solution. For example:

"If you don't _____, *then you will* _____.*"*

(When making this point you casually and naturally move to the bad/negative location.)

"But if you do take heed and _____, *you will* _____.*"*

(In this case you move, again casually and naturally, to the good/positive location.)

2. *To create a timeline—the past, present, and future—when you are sequencing events.*

Split the platform into thirds in your mind's eye. Consider the audience's left your past location, the middle of the stage the present, and the audience's right the future location. (Reason for this: In western culture, we read from left to right, and as speakers, we always work in the audience's favor, not in our own.)

Say, in the *past* location, "If you could have seen me four months ago, you would have seen ..."

Say, moving to the *present* location, "Right at this moment, I ..."

Say, moving to the *future* position, "Now fast-forward three years ..." or "And over the next two decades, I ..." or "In the future, I would like to move toward ..."

3. *To differentiate between points.*

Designate a spot on the stage for each point/idea within your speech and when you want to change points or ideas, demonstrate this with physical transitions from one location to the next. Move at such points in your speech as:

"On the other hand ..."

"Having said that, there is another point ..."

"Similarly, this other story ..."

Where you move in these cases is irrelevant; you simply need to demonstrate your transition visually.

When you tell stories, change locations as you create different scenes with characters, dialogue, and actions. This will help your listeners remember and differentiate between one event/story/point and others as they visualize these scenes.

At the end, when you refer to something you have already said, just call it back by pointing or gesturing to the spot where you previously spoke about it. Doing this will evoke emotion in your audience; they will be able to see in their minds the story you talked about at that location.

By creating a lasting picture of an experience, you have engaged the audience's senses. (This includes smell and touch, as, for instance, when you describe the aroma of baking a chocolate cake or the feel of a soft cushiony carpet.)

A speaker's main reason to speak is to create change in an audience. Change occurs through emotional, not intellectual, means. When you wish to stress an important point in your speech and move your audience to action, tap into their emotions. *Stop* and remain there; then pause, lower your voice, and slow down to deliver your power statement.

You can motivate an audience to change through this process, grounding them and giving them time to reflect and realize the process/point/message being stated.

I challenge you to move with purpose on the platform. Neither remain glued to the spot nor wander aimlessly.

When you move, move *mindfully*.

You—the Most Important Word in Speaking

"THE YOU-TURN."

—DAVID BROOKS,
1995 WORLD CHAMPION OF PUBLIC SPEAKING

"I-YOU RATIO."

—PATRICIA FRIPP, CSP, CPAE,
SPEAKER AND AUTHOR

"THE YOU-FOCUS."

—CRAIG VALENTINE,
1999 WORLD CHAMPION OF PUBLIC SPEAKING

Y es, *you*.

Have you ever slept through almost the whole of a speaker's presentation? You weren't engaged by the speaker and you thought: "So what? Who cares? What's in it for me?"

In contrast, have you ever been captivated by a speaker from beginning to end?

What's the difference that makes the difference? Which tools did the latter speaker use to **connect** with your own individual, unique thoughts and emotions?

PROMISE: Picking up this simple yet significant strategy of using "you" in your speeches will put you strides ahead of other speakers because you'll know how to connect with and engage your audience from start to close.

ROADMAP: You will discover:

- When to use *you*, the most important word in speaking

- Why to use it

- How to use it

Connection, Connection, Connection

Have you ever heard a speaker say:

"How many of you ...?"

"Has anyone here ...?"

"All of you may know that ..."

"Does everyone/anyone know ...?"

"Who knows ...?"

Some of you may say ..."

"Those of you who have ..."

When you hear those kinds of questions, to whom is the speaker speaking? *Everyone* ... yet, in fact, **no one**.

A speaker needs to connect with each individual audience member. How can this be accomplished when we have a large group in front of us?

Imagine you are having a conversation with someone. Would you go up to him or her and say: "How many of you have ...?"

No, you would say: "Have you ever ...?"

You can apply those same words to an entire group: "Have you ever ...?" This is a powerful practice.

"Speak to *one*, yet Look to *all*," says Craig Valentine.

Speak to one with your content while looking to all with your eyes.

Using this important process, you can create a one-on-one connection with your audience so each member of it can say: "Wow—the speaker is speaking directly to me." How? By speaking to one person with your content through the use of the word "you," while looking to everyone with your eyes.

To sell your point, have each person hearing "you" at "hello" and also at "goodbye." **Connect** with your audience **before**, **during**, and **at the end** of your presentation.

Why Use *You* at the Start of Your Presentation

- Gets their attention

- Makes them curious and excited to join you on your journey

- Helps them hear a benefit for themselves because they know the focus is on *them*

Why Use *You* During Your Presentation

- Gives audience members opportunities to reflect on their own lives

- Allows you to touch base with them periodically as you would in conversation

- Draws on similarities between you and the audience; it

avoids making you appear "special"

- Invites them into your stories/scenes in a visual, auditory, and kinesthetic way

Why Use *You* at the Close of Your Presentation

- Recaps the you-focused benefit

- Helps audience buy into your point and take action

How to Use *You* at the Start of Your Presentations

- Tap into their world—ask a you-focused question

- Give them a you-focused statement and/or a you-focused benefit in terms of what they will definitely receive by listening to you:

    "In the next few minutes, you will pick up/hear/discover/ receive/get ..."

    "Raise your hand if ..."

"It may interest you to know that ..."

"Did you/have you ever ...?"

"When was the last time you ...?"

"Did you know that ...?"

How to Use *You* During Your Presentation

- Transport them into your world with your stories, which will include you-focused questions—and you-focused statements:

  "Can you relate to that?"

  "As an (adult, engineer, parent, etc.), you know that ..."

  "And as you likely can relate ..."

  "If, like me, you own a house, you may have experienced ..."

  "I don't know about you but I ..."

  "Had you been swimming with me in that cool ocean water, you would have seen ..."

"I wish you had been there because you would have heard ..."

How to Use *You* During the Close of Your Presentation

For example:

"When you explore and try new things, you'll be amazed at the joy of life you'll experience because of the talents you have discovered."

"If you choose to adopt a consistent positive outlook, you will be surprised to see how many friends you'll gain because people will naturally be attracted to you."

When you use this slight yet profound strategy of using the most important connecting word **you** in your statements and questions, your audience will want to journey with you throughout your entire speech.

Why? Because the focus is on *them*, not on you the speaker.

GET YOURSELF INTO
THE SPEAKING ZONE

"Do not dwell in
the past, do not
dream of the future,
concentrate the mind
on the present moment."

–Buddha

Both the speaker and the audience share a degree of anxiety and apprehension at the beginning of a presentation.

That said, would you choose to be stressed as a speaker if you knew you had the option not to be?

> **PROMISE:** By following the suggested environmental, physical, and mental preparation tips before your speech, you will *zone* into your audience more easily, allowing you to be more real and comfortable and connect with them more readily.

> **ROADMAP:** We will look at a few characteristics of speakers who are *in the zone* and how you can *get into the zone*.

The desired state for a speaker before and during a speech is to be totally present and in the moment. In other words, to be *in the zone*.

Characteristics of a Speaker Who's in the Zone

- Calm, centered, confident

- Focuses with total concentration on the present

- Real and authentic (speaking more from the heart than from the head)

- More passionate about content and desire to help others

- Grounded in the reality of the moment—able to think on one's feet easily and be more spontaneous and creative in responses to the audience

- Playful and energetic

Are there any other characteristics you can think of or have experienced?

How You Can Get into (and Stay in) the Zone

Prepare Your Environment

- Check out the room, including the seating arrangements. Will everyone be able to see and hear you?

- Are there any barriers between you and the audience that you need to remove?

- Is the room temperature comfortable for the audience?

- Are there too many chairs, which may leave the front rows empty? (Remove back ones, if necessary)

- Have you established a friendly working relationship with the AV person?

Prepare Yourself Physically

- Don't eat for an hour and a half before you speak

- Avoid ice cold drinks, caffeine

- Keep throat moist with room temperature water

- Meet and greet your audience as they come in

- Use calming breath exercises

Prepare Yourself Mentally

- Minimize personal worries. Rather, as Darren LaCroix, 2001 World Champion of Public Speaking, puts it: "Worry bigger ... not about yourself but about the audience. It's all about them, not you, the speaker."

- Think about the message the audience will take with them. What do you want them to think, say, or do differently after you're finished speaking?

- Visualize a great presentation

- Listen to an empowering song or one you just really like

- Remind yourself to have fun; if you need to, place a note in your pocket prompting you to do so

Zone in on Your Audience When You're Being Introduced

- Providing the person who is introducing you with a great introduction is another way to help you zone into the moment with your audience. Recheck the chapter about introductions (pages 67–73) so you can avoid the following scenario.

Have you ever heard a speaker being introduced and thought: "So what! Who cares? What's in it for me?" Unfortunately, many speakers write introductions that turn audiences off even *before* they begin their speech proper.

- Create a connection with your audiences and zone in even before you get to the body of your speech. Try to inject some humor into your introduction. This can help you gage your audience's energy level and establish a connection with them

- What methods will you use in order to get *into the zone* with your audience? Do the above and the butterflies may still flutter, but at least they'll be flying in formation

CONCLUSION

Now that you've read this book's tips, formulas, and suggestions, you can become a more powerful presenter, one who knows how to create a memorable message and connect effectively with your audience. You now have the tools and techniques to give you a competitive advantage in the workplace, helping you talk your way to the top; or, if you are a toastmaster, the tools and techniques to excel in speech competitions.

Regardless of your reason for seeking enhanced verbal communication skills, you should know that powerful and effective speaking is a process that can be learned. Understanding and utilizing the content in this book, combined with a great deal of practice in front of audiences, will help you become a more confident, conversational communicator.

Yes, you can go . . .

from dull to DYNAMIC

from boring to BRILLIANT

from good to GREAT

from a wannabe speaker to a WORLD CLASS SPEAKER

If you're not a toastmaster, find a club near you (visit: www. toastmasters.org). Being part of a club will enhance your confidence as a speaker, which, in turn, will elevate your personal and professional life, as has been the case for me.

If you, like me, want to learn more—that is, beyond the resources and assistance of a Toastmasters club—then attend seminars on advanced skills. If you're coached by world class coaches, a certification I was pleased to earn recently, you will be guaranteed to receive education, not just validation. Check my website for my own seminars (www. kathrynmackenzie.com).

Want to step forward even farther? Please click on the RESOURCES page on my site www.kathrynmackenzie.com and check the World Champions of Public Speaking resources and Champ Camps.

In closing, let me ask, How important is it to speak with excellence? No one has answered the question better than Daniel Webster, who said: "If all my possessions were taken from me with one exception, I would choose to keep the power of speech, for by it I would soon regain all the rest."

ABOUT THE AUTHOR

KATHRYN MACKENZIE, M.ED.

Kathryn MacKenzie was born and raised for her first 12 years on the island of Malta and then moved with her family to Canada. Never did this petite, blonde, pigtailed, shy little girl dream that she would ever stand on a speaking platform, go on to teach others to speak with confidence, and even write a book on the subject. Kathryn taught elementary and high school for most of her adult life. During that time, she was selected as a school board education consultant for six years and worked directly with teaching staffs. Her degrees and other specialist courses were completed while she was a full-time educator. She received her bachelor of arts degree from the University of Waterloo, Ontario, and her master of education degree from OISE at the University of Toronto.

After retiring from teaching, Kathryn discovered Toastmasters. Her club members encouraged her to pursue speaking and this she did with a vengeance. She is now an award-winning speaker and certified world class speaking coach and presentation skills instructor. Kathryn has spoken in Canada and in several U.S. states, including Alaska. Called an "edutaining professor with pizzazz" by her former college students, to whom she taught Speaking with Confidence, Kathryn has incorporated passion, energy, and humor into her personal and professional life.

Her eclectic background as an educator, education consultant, and part-time hobby stage actress for over 25 years has provided her with ongoing opportunities to facilitate growth in others while at the same time exercising both a dynamic stage presence and superior instructing skills. For the past seven years, she has been studying the art of speaking with the World Champions of Public Speaking.

Kathryn has always believed that all people have magnificence within them but has noted that unfortunately all too often they do not tap into it, leaving so many speeches unmade, books unwritten, songs unsung, and talents never discovered. She has made it her mission to help others, through her speeches and writing, to magnify their magnificence. She is thrilled that she has witnessed both of her children, Christopher and Carolyn, now adults, magnify their own magnificence by excelling in fulfilling their God-given talents. Kathryn hopes to see their children, her grandchildren, continue to do the same in their lives.

In her keynotes and seminars, Kathryn empowers people to take action to achieve their unique potential, whether it is in speaking skills or life in general. Drawing from her own life experiences, she delivers personal and professional poignancy in an entertaining, enlightening, and energetic manner.

To book Kathryn as a speaking coach, presentation skills instructor, keynote speaker, or seminar facilitator, contact her at: **kathryn@kathrynmackenzie.com**

Visit her website, **www.kathrynmackenzie.com**, for more information about her programs, recommended resources, and free monthly newsletter on speaking skills: *Keys to Speaking Success*.